THE GREAT
LIGHT, LEAN
AND LOW FAT
COOKBOOK

Colour Library

THE GREAT
LIGHT, LEAN
AND LOW FAT
COOKBOOK

CONTENTS

INTRODUCED BY FELICITY SALTER
PHOTOGRAPHED BY PETER BARRY
RECIPES STYLED BY HELEN BURDETT
DESIGNED BY ALISON JEWELL AND SALLY STRUGNELL
JACKET DESIGN BY ROGER HYDE
EDITED BY JILLIAN STEWART

4948
This edition published in 1996 by Colour Library Direct
© 1991 CLB International, Godalming, Surrey
All rights reserved
Printed and bound in Singapore by Tien Wah Press
ISBN 1-85833-596-5

What is healthy eating?

It seems that for every authority that tells you to eat more of some food, another tells you not to bother…fat is bad, eat oily fish, cut down on sugar, eat dried apricots, bananas are bad for you, don't eat bread, eat jacket potatoes, etc., etc. Clearly, as the awareness of healthy eating increases, it also becomes harder to sort out all the advice and differing opinions.

The importance of exercise

Although this book is particularly concerned with sensible eating, it is important to remember that health, diet and fitness are all linked. No matter how conscientious you are with your food, you'll also need to take regular exercise. It's best to aim to exercise at least 2 or 3 times a week for approximately 30 minutes each time. Take things gradually though, if you haven't exercised for some time. Start by trying to walk on a frequent basis rather than taking the car. Make the effort to walk up stairs rather than being lazy and always opting for the lift. When you become more fit you can then try running up the stairs. Once you have mastered that, try and join a gym or class and make exercise a natural part of your life. You may like to take up jogging – but seek your doctor's approval before starting. Keeping fit by taking regular exercise not only makes you feel better, but you'll find that you actually have more energy too. It will also mean that your metabolic rate – that is basically the rate at which your body uses food – will increase. So you'll tend not to store fat, but use it.

Of course, there are other factors affecting

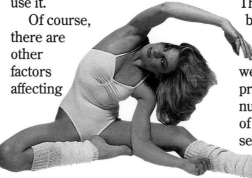

Regular exercise is very beneficial.

health apart from diet and exercise, such as heredity illnesses and smoking. There is little point eating and exercising conscientiously if you are still smoking – so give up! Taking care of your health through diet and exercise isn't just a case of adding a few more years onto your life span, one in 3 deaths in people over 35 could be postponed by making changes to the diet, and far more people would enjoy an active and healthy life well into old age, if they lived a healthier lifestyle.

Variety is the key to a healthy diet.

A balanced diet explained

The belief in the value of a balanced diet grew out of the realisation that if a large enough variety of foods were consumed, this would prevent deficiencies in any nutrients. Ironically, it is our lack of ability to choose our foods sensibly from the enormous range available, that has helped to cause some of today's health problems:

• Heart disease kills about 180,000 people in Britain each year

• By middle age 50% of men and 30% of women are too fat

So if variety is the key to good health, it is essential to understand the elements which contribute to a healthy eating plan.

No single food can provide adequate amounts of all protein, fats, carbohydrates, vitamins and minerals necessary to maintain health and vitality. Therefore it is crucial to choose a variety of foods that not only taste good, but also provide the right balance of nutrients. It is the 'balance' and the selection and combination of foods chosen which will help you to avoid eating too much of some foods, whilst ensuring that the nutrients you require are then consumed in adequate amounts.

The following chart explains what the essential nutrients are, in which foods they may be found and their role in the body. A report by the National Advisory Commitee on Nutrition Education (Nacne) made a number of recommendations

NUTRIENT	IMPORTANT SOURCES OF NUTRIENT	SOME MAJOR FUNCTIONS	
		BUILDING & MAINTENANCE	REGULATORY PROCESSES
PROTEIN	Meat, poultry, fish, pulses, eggs, cheese, milk, nuts.	Promotes growth and repair of tissues. Forms structure of every cell, such as muscle, blood, bone, skin, hair, nails. Maintains healthy body cells.	Makes up part of enzymes, some hormones and body fluids and the antibodies which increase resistance to infection.
CARBOHYDRATE	Bread, cereal, sugar, potatoes, beans.	Supplies energy and can be used for growth and maintenance of body cells.	Unrefined products supply fibre to promote regular bowel movement.
FAT	Butter, margarine, oil, milk, cheese, fatty meats.	Most concentrated source of energy. Constitutes part of structure of every cell. Supplies essential fatty acids.	Provides and carries fat-soluble vitamins A, D, E and K.
VITAMINS	Fresh fruit and vegetables, dairy produce, nuts, liver, kidney.	Increases resistance to infection. Strengthens blood vessels, healing wounds and bones.	Regulates metabolic processes.
MINERALS CALCIUM	Milk, yogurt, bread, cheese, cereals, sardines, canned salmon (with bones), green vegetables, citrus fruits, pulses.	Combines with other minerals to give structure and strength to bones and teeth.	
IRON	Liver, kidneys, red meat, bread, potatoes, egg yolk, green vegetables, pulses, cereals.	Combines with protein to form haemoglobin, the red substance in blood that carries oxygen and carbon dioxide to the cells.	Functions as part of enzymes in tissue respiration.
SODIUM	Salt, salt found in foods such as bacon, ham, smoked fish, cheese, butter, margarine and most other processed food.		Maintains water balance in the body.
POTASSIUM	Milk, fruit juice, bananas, dried fruits, meat, bran, peanut butter, pulses, potatoes.	Helps release of energy from carbohydrates, proteins and fats.	Required for muscle contraction.
MAGNESIUM	Green vegetables (raw), nuts especially almonds and cashews, soya beans, seeds, wholegrains.	Building bones and manufacturing proteins.	Helps functioning of nerves.
PHOSPHORUS	Milk, cheese, yogurt, wholemeal bread other cereals, malt, fish, eggs, vegetables.	Maintains healthy bones. Important for energy release.	
ZINC	Meat, liver, eggs, poultry, seafood, milk, wholegrains.	Growth and synthesis of proteins, wound healing, aids sexual maturation. Maintenance of hair, nails and mucous membranes.	Required for normal functioning of thyroid gland.
IODINE	Seafood, iodized salt, sea salt.		Essential for maintaining normal metabolism in all the body's cells.
FLUORINE	Fish, tea, drinking water, toothpaste.	Formation of healthy bones and teeth and resistance to dental decay.	

after looking at the average British diet. They advised that fat intakes should be reduced by 25%, to provide not more than 30% of our total energy intake. Saturated fatty acid intake should be, on average, not more than 10% of the total energy intake.

Average sucrose intake should be reduced by approximately 50% to 20kg per head per year. Of this, not more than 10kg should be derived from snack foods.

Fibre intake should be increased by 33% to 30g per head per day. The increase should come mainly from greater consumption of wholegrain cereals.

Salt should be reduced by approximately 25% to no more than 9g per head per day.

No recommendations either to increase or decrease total protein intake have been made. Other recommendations, would however, ensure a greater proportion of protein being consumed from vegetable sources.

The energy content of the diet should be sufficient for individuals to maintain optimum body weight and allow adequate exercise.

There were also recommendations to moderate alcohol consumption and not to smoke.

Looking back

Many years ago man hunted for food, feasted, then spent several days searching for the next meal. Fat was invaluable then, as it was stored to provide a reserve source of energy. Today, however, food is abundant and we don't go for days without eating – therefore our reserve fat store remains. We are also generally less active than our predecessors – so as a result fat is stored and builds up to become excess weight. Most of us eat too much fat and because it provides more energy (calories) weight for weight, than other foods, it is often one of the major causes of obesity. In fact, it is not just a case of how much fat we eat, we should also be concerned with the sort of fat.

What are the different types of fat in food?

The most common form of fat, making up approximately 98% of that present in the body, is termed neutral fat, or triglycerides. These fats, or triglycerides are made up of fatty acids and glycerol in a ratio 3:1 respectively. Usually a proportion of each of the three basic categories of fatty acids, (saturated, mono-unsaturated and polyunsaturated) exist but one type of fatty acid predominates. The type of fat will depend on the relative quantities of these fatty acids and will then be classified as saturated, mono-unsaturated or polyunsaturated.

Saturated fats

These contain a majority of saturated fatty acids, or saturates and are usually solid at room temperature. Foods rich in saturated fat are nearly always of animal origin. The exceptions to this are coconut and palm oil. Butter, lard, cream, wholemilk, cheese, suet and visible meat fats are typical, but margarine and hydrogenated vegetables oils are also examples of saturated fats. Saturated fats can increase blood cholesterol level, and for those susceptible, this in turn can be a contributory factor in heart disease.

Polyunsaturated fats

These are rich in polyunsaturated acids and are generally liquid or very soft at room temperature and when refrigerated. They are usually of vegetable origin, although fish oils break this rule, being high in polyunsaturated fatty acids.

The main sources of polyunsaturated fat include: corn, safflower, sunflower, groundnut and rapeseed oils, and polyunsaturated margarine. Polyunsaturated fats can lower the blood cholesterol level.

Mono-unsaturated fats

These contain fatty acids which are mainly mono-unsaturated in nature. They are soft or liquid at room temperature, but may solidify in cold temperatures. The most well known source is olive oil, but it is also present in the fat of poultry and oily fish such as mackerel, herring and salmon.

So to clarify, it is important to understand that no single food contains only one sort of fat; it is the proportion to which varying fats are present, which distinguishes the different foods.

Cooking fat for example,

contains ten times as much saturated fat as it does polyunsaturated, whereas, wholewheat bread has twice as much polyunsaturated fat as saturated.

A note about margarines

Some people are under the misconception that margarines are better for you than butter, although this may often not be the case.

Several margarine manufacturers start with cheap ingredients such as beef suet or whale oil and then rely on extensive processing, colouring or additions to produce a palatable result.

They also use a process known as hydrogenation which solidifies fat, but in turn alters unsaturated fats into saturated fats. So look out for margarines made from cold pressed unsaturated oils (which have not been hydrogenated) in health food shops.

Cholesterol in Food

Meat	Mg per 100g
Brains	2200
Liver	260-43
Lean duck breast	160
Lamb, lean	110
Beef, lean	82
Chicken, breast	74
Turkey, breast	62

Dairy products	Mg per 100g
Egg yolk	1260
Egg, whole	450
Butter	230
Parmesan cheese	90
Edam cheese	72
Cheddar cheese	70
Milk, whole	14
Milk, skimmed	2
Egg white	0

Fish	Mg per 100g
Prawns	200
Fish, white	70
Fish, oily	80

Miscellaneous	
Lard	70+
Margarine (from animal fat)	65
Margarine (from vegetable fat)	0
Vegetables & cereals	0

What is cholesterol?

Cholesterol is a fat-like substance which is produced in the bodies of all animals, including man. Animal foods will therefore contain some cholesterol, whereas foods of vegetable origin contain very little, if any. Cholesterol is an important body constituent required for normal day to day functioning of the body.

Functions of cholesterol:

• Forms part of cell membranes and protects nerve fibres
• Involved in the manufacture of hormones, particularly sex hormones and those which regulate the body's digestive system

Cholesterol is a constituent of Vitamin D which is manufactured by the body from the action of sunlight on the body. But you don't need very much – everyday the body manufactures

approximately 1g of cholesterol and it makes a further 0.5g from the diet. The body actually produces four times more than it needs, so there is no risk of a cholesterol deficiency.

Cholesterol is transported around the body in the bloodstream and some people have a tendency to lay down an excess of cholesterol as fatty deposits in the blood vessels. If the body doesn't process this properly, it will build up year by year to such an extent that the cholesterol levels become dangerously high. The heart then has to work exceptionally hard to pump the blood through.

Since saturated fats can increase blood cholesterol, it is therefore best to keep consumption low.

Many of the so called diseases of civilisation such as cancer, heart disease, high blood pressure, obesity and diverticulitis are becoming increasingly linked with high cholesterol diets.

As long ago as 1916, studies comparing the low fat diets of the Japanese to the cholesterol-rich diets of northern Europe and America, found a high correlation between high fat, low fibre, Western diets and cancer and heart disease.

However, no conclusive evidence has evolved relating dietary cholesterol to raised blood cholesterol levels. Nevertheless, a diet high in saturated fatty acids is believed to raise the blood cholesterol levels, whereas, polyunsaturated fatty acids may reduce the level.

It is believed that reducing our total fat intake, especially of saturated fat, should have long term benefits and may help to reduce the risk of ill health. Medical experts are therefore advising that we should:

• Reduce total fat in the diet
• Limit saturated fat intake to approximately ⅓ of the total fat in the diet, replacing saturated fat with polyunsaturated fat as much as possible

Why eat less fat?

Apart from the need to eat less saturated fat to reduce the risks of high blood cholesterol levels, bare in mind the following points:

• Half the fat we eat is surplus to the fat we need
• Although we need some fat in our diet for energy and to supply the essential fat soluble vitamins, we do need to reduce our intake (on average an adult needs no more than 75g/3oz of fat each day)
• Fat contains over 200 calories per 25g (1oz). Therefore, a high fat diet will certainly be high in calories and as a result will encourage weight gain
• You are what you eat, so it makes sense to eat less fat

Avoiding fats

This can be very difficult unless you make everything yourself, and although it is nice to, we don't always have the time. A surprising number of processed foods tend to contain fats, so read labels carefully, and remember that ingredients are listed in order of importance.

This leaves the fat present in natural foods. These may contain fat, but also have a high food value. Eggs for example have approximately 11% total fat content, raw, boiled or poached, yet they are also a good source of protein and vitamins.

Practical ways to cut down on fat

• Eat more meat-free meals
• When buying meat, choose lean cuts
• Trim off visible fat from all meat
• Remove skin from poultry
• Replace full cream milk with skimmed (except for young children)
• Use low fat fromage frais or natural yogurt instead of cream
• Eat fruit flavoured, low fat fromage frais, instead of mousses or soufflés
• Have sorbet instead of ice cream
• Have fresh fruit salads instead of spongey puddings
• Replace full fat cheese e.g. Cheddar and Stilton with medium fat cheeses, such as Brie or Camembert or eat low fat cheeses, such as cottage cheese
• Use low calorie salad dressings instead of mayonnaise
• Spread sandwiches with reduced calorie dressings, instead of butter
• Replace cream-filled cakes and chocolate biscuits with wholemeal alternatives
• Garnish jacket potatoes with chives and natural yogurt instead of butter
• Instead of deep frying, shallow fry or roast without additional fat
• If shallow frying, always make sure that the fat is thoroughly preheated, so that the fat absorbed into the food is minimised
• Boil, bake, grill and poach where possible
• Cook with non-stick pans to reduce the amount of fat needed
• Use gentle heats when using unsaturated fats, since they can change into saturated fats during cooking

What is dietary fibre?

It is a form of carbohydrate which is naturally present in foods of plant origin – that includes fruit, vegetables, pulses, cereals and seeds. It is what makes up the skeleton of plants, the husks of grains, the shells of beans and the skins of fruit and vegetables. For many years this part of foods was considered superfluous and because it often gave food a chewier texture it was often refined away e.g. brown flour was refined to produce white flour.

Fibre values are therefore often reduced by processing or refining, yet they are also reduced in cooking too. Take, for example, a fresh apple – this contains approximately 1.8g of dietary fibre to each 100g. If cooked and made into apple purée, this reduces dietary fibre to 1.5g per 100g. This is reduced even further when made into apple juice – when it no longer contains any fibre.

Why do we need fibre?

Fibre is made up of complex carbohydrates which cannot be

digested by the body and for this reason, it was considered of no dietary value for many years.

Recent research linked insufficient fibre in the diet with a whole range of disorders, such as diverticulosis, haemorrhoids, gallstones and varicose veins, as well as conditions as serious as heart disease, diabetes and cancer of the colon. These complaints, often called diseases of affluence, are all relatively common in Western societies, where diets, are often low in fibre. In comparison to developing countries, where diets are high in fibre, the same problems do not appear to occur.

How much fibre should we be eating?

Expert opinion is united in recommending that people consume more fibre. The Nacne report, for instance, recommends aiming for 30g (just over 1oz) each day. The current UK average is 20g, although some individuals eat as little as 6g.

The easiest way to eat more fibre, is to eat more unrefined foods – remembering that only plant foods have fibre. The recipes in this book use a good balance of foods high in fibre, from cereals and nuts, to fruit and vegetables.

Is it possible to eat too much fibre?

Fibre in the diet should be increased gradually. Too much, too quickly, can cause stomach ache. Fibre can have a laxative effect and large amounts of insoluble fibre may cause

excessive flatulence, and an initial bloating feeling, due to the water it absorbs in the stomach. So the rule is to adapt your diet slowly, and you'll benefit in both the short and long term. For example, change to wholemeal bread this week, then add a piece of fruit with skin on, each day. Introduce wholegrain cereals and try making pastry, scones etc. with ½ wholemeal flour and ½ white flour. In the next month, try adding beans and lentils to casseroles, then slowly introduce dried fruits and nuts.

Many everyday foods contain fibre.

Role of salt in the body

Salt is a naturally occuring compound made up of sodium and chloride, hence the name sodium chloride. Approximately 10% of sodium is found in tissue cells, 40% is present in bone cells and the remaining 50% is located outside the cells in the body fluids.

Sodium is needed for nerve and muscle functioning, and to maintain the fluid balance mechanism. It is also a major factor in determining blood pressure. Chlorine plays an important part in digestion, because it is a major element in the acid present in our stomachs and like sodium, it is essential for the correct functioning of the nervous system.

The need for water and salt is closely linked. Too little salt may result in muscular cramps, whereas high salt intakes, are likely to cause a feeling of thirst. Loss of fluid through perspiration results in the concentration of sodium increasing in the remaining body fluid, which consequently makes you thirsty. Salt is therefore an essential dietary requirement in small quantities.

The functions of salt

For many years, man has used salt as a preservative, in cured meats for example. It is an important textural agent in many manufactured foods, whilst it is equally necessary in making basic foods such as bread and cheese. However, we are most familiar with it's function as a flavour enhancer.

The disadvantages of salt

In theory, surplus salt should be excreted via the kidneys. In practice, some people's kidneys do this more efficiently than others. Too much salt creates extra work for the kidneys and may result in excess fluid retention. This can sometimes be seen as swelling of the face, hands or ankles, and can cause a rise in blood pressure. In those vulnerable to high blood pressure, eating too much salt leads to a higher risk of a heart attack or stroke. This link between high blood pressure and salt was established as long ago as 1928.

High Sodium Foods

bacon,
baking powder and bicarbonate of soda, bread unless homemade without salt,
biscuits (savoury),
butter unless unsalted,
cereals for breakfast – almost all apart from oats, muesli and unprocessed flaked varieties,
cheese, except a few labelled low sodium or homemade cheese,
convenience foods (most)
crisps
kippers and cured fish
Indian meals
low fat spreads
margarines, unless low salt
nuts, salted e.g. peanuts
olives
pastry, unless made with unsalted fat
salad dressings
sausages
pies filled with meat
burgers
self-raising flour
shellfish
smoked meats
soups, tinned, dried
soy sauce
stock cubes
tinned vegetables
yeast extract

Low Sodium Foods

barley
beans
cream
egg yolks
fruit
honey
lentils (cooked)
mustard (dry)
nuts (unsalted)
oats
pasta
potatoes
rabbit
rice
rye
sugar
wheat
soya flour
vegetable oils
wheat germ

Avoid Processed Foods

Most of the salt we eat comes from processed foods. Canned vegetables for example, have 200 times more salt than the fresh ones. So as you can see in the list of high sodium foods, it's not just the obvious foods you have to watch. Many food additives are based on sodium. However, they are generally present in each item in relatively small proportions, so they should not be a cause for concern in themselves. It is the accumulation of many processed foods which causes a problem. Look out for the increasing range of products that are now sold optionally without salt, such as canned sweetcorn.

Manufactured foods tend to have a far higher proportion of sodium. Natural foods, by comparison, contain either roughly equal amounts of sodium and potassium, or they are higher in potassium. It is important to try and maintain the correct sodium/ potassium balance in the body, and excess salt can disrupt this.

Getting the balance right

Most of us find food without any salt bland and uninteresting. However, we tend to eat salt mainly out of habit and it is possible to adapt the taste buds in just a few weeks to want less salt.

Steps to reducing salt intake

• Limit foods containing high levels of salt
• Reduce or omit the addition of salt at the table
• Restrict the amount of salt added during cooking

If you find it difficult to reduce salt you may find it helpful to use alternative flavourings to cushion the change in taste.

Alternative Flavourings

WITH BEEF	horseradish, ginger, black pepper, French mustard
WITH CHICKEN	lemon juice, garlic, paprika, coriander, cumin
WITH LAMB	mint, rosemary, chilli powder, garlic, turmeric, lemon juice

WITH PORK	orange juice, ginger, garlic, spring onions
WITH FISH	black pepper, lemon juice, parsley, dill
WITH POTATOES	chives, spring onions, dill, parsley, tumeric
WITH RICE	saffron, garlic, onion, coconut
WITH GREEN BEANS	lemon juice, mustard seeds
WITH PEAS	mint, parsley, onions
WITH CARROTS	orange juice, coriander, chives
WITH TOMATOES	basil, oregano, marjoram

When making your own bread without salt, overcome the bland flavour by mixing the dough with buttermilk instead of water. Add additional flavourings such as sesame seeds, roasted

Avoid sugary cakes and desserts.

sunflower seeds or caraway seeds.

You can also make your own baking powder by mixing equal parts of arrowroot, cream of tartar and potassium bicarbonate, (your pharmacist may well make this up for you).

All about sugar

There are many types of sugar available in foods, not just table sugar, which can be in the form of granulated, caster or icing sugar. Sugar is the term given to a group of carbohydrate substances.

Glucose - this is sometimes referred to as grape sugar, dextrose or corn syrup. It occurs naturally in many foods including grapes, corn and other fruit and vegetables.

Glucose is the basic unit of which all other sugars are composed, and to which most sugars and starches are broken down to by the body.

Fructose - this is also called fruit sugar. Sold in packets, it also exists naturally in fruit, many vegetables and honey. It is the sweetest of all common sugars.

Sucrose - this can be in the form of caster, granulated, icing, brown and muscovado sugar. It may be obtained from sugar beet or sugar cane. Sucrose from sugar beet needs to be manufactured to remove the bitter tasting molasses.

Lactose - this is naturally present in milk.

All white sugar is refined. However, it may then be ground and coloured, so sugar which is brown is not necessarily unrefined. It is believed that unrefined sugar contains small quantities of minerals. Nevertheless, they are present in such tiny amounts that they are of no significance.

This is why sugar has been omitted from the sugar-free section of the book and many of the recipes rely on natural sweetness or the addition of naturally sweet foods for flavour.

Sugar in manufactured foods

Apart from the sugar that you consciously add to foods, sugar is also contained in many manufactured foods. Approximately 60% of the sugar consumed in the U.K. is taken in in this way.

Sugar is a food manufacturer's delight, offering tastiness, shelf-life and texture, all at low cost. Many foods that are considered savoury contain sugar e.g. pickle is 30% sugar, chutney is 50%

whereas jam is 60%.

Although sales of sugar in packets has declined, sugar consumption as a whole has not, due to the fact that between 60-75% of the sugar we eat comes from manufactured foods. Coke for example contains 35ml (7tsps) sugar per glass. Just think how you would cringe if someone wanted that much sugar in their tea!

It is also the frequency at which these sugar-rich foods are consumed that is causing concern. It is this frequency which is believed to have the greatest effect on dental decay. If you have to indulge in sugary foods, it is preferable to confine it to the occasional treat.

How much sugar should we consume?

Excess sugar can lead to 2 main problems - firstly being overweight and secondly, dental decay.

It is currently estimated that we consume 100g (4oz) of sugar per day. This figure represents an estimated total consumption - that is table sugar plus sugar present in prepared food.

The Nacne report says that the ideal diet would contain no sucrose, however, the maximum intake to meet recommendations should not be greater than 50g (2oz) a day from any source.

Why eat less sugar?

• Refined sugar contains no nutrients, only calories (although less refined sugars contain some trace elements, they are only available in minimum amounts - much less than the value of most foods)
• Sugar contains 100 calories per 25g or 110 per oz, so it is extremely high in 'empty' calories. These calories would be better 'spent' on foods providing minerals, vitamins and fibre
• Calories from sugar are quickly absorbed and therefore encourage weight gain
• Sugar is a principal factor in tooth decay (brushing the teeth only makes a marginal difference)
• Too much sugar increases the levels of fats (triglycerides) in the blood and particularly increases the fats which may be associated with circulatory complaints
• In some children, high sugar intake can result in hyperactivity
• Sugar is a drain on nutrients, especially B vitamins and calcium
• Whilst sugar is high in calories, it is not satisfying. It is therefore easy to eat a lot. An average day's consumption of 100g (4oz) is 400 calories. To eat the same amount of calories in other foods, you would have to eat your way through 500g (1lb 2oz) peeled bananas or 900g (2½lbs) of apples or 450g (1lb) of potatoes
• It drastically raises blood sugar levels

Does sugar give you energy?

In theory sugar does provide energy, but there is more to it than that. Whatever you eat raises your blood sugar level to some extent, and provided that glucose is released slowly during digestion, this blood sugar level is maintained. This sustains mental and physical ability, helping to keep our emotions balanced.

When we eat unrefined high fibre carbohydrate, such as wholemeal bread, everything is fine, because it is digested slowly.

However, a concentrated supply of refined sugar is absorbed quickly, and this raises blood sugar to very high levels. In response to this, the pancreas sends insulin to lower the sugar level, causing a rapid fall, which causes another craving for sugar. So a vicious circle is set up causing bursts of energy, followed by fatigue.

Foods high in added sugars

Marmalade, jam, chocolate, sweets, soft drinks including fizzy drinks, sweet biscuits especially chocolate, sweetened breakfast cereals, puddings, cakes, meringues, mousses, jellies, sweet liqueurs, pickles, chutneys, sauces, ketchup, canned fruit in syrup

Making the most of natural sugars

It may well be difficult to initially reduce sugar intake, so take things gradually as a means of making foods acceptable.

Within the low sugar section of this book the best possible use has been made of naturally sweet foods, as a means of sweetening varying foods. These include honey, and dried fruits such as apricots, currant, dates, figs, prunes, raisins and sultanas. Nevertheless, although naturally sweet, they should not be eaten in excess.

In the early stages of sugar reduction, try using ³/₄ of the sugar you would normally add to drinks. You can gradually reduce these when this established new level has become normal and enjoyable.

The essential vitamins

The human body is a sophisticated machine which needs many elements to keep it running efficiently. Apart from protein, carbohydrates, fats and minerals the body also needs a good supply of vitamins.

Vitamins contribute to good health, by enabling the body to function at its best. They are responsible for growth

Fresh fruit is a good alternative to sticky desserts.

and repair of body tissues, for healthy skin, good vision, strong bones and good teeth.

Vitamins do not supply the body with any energy, although some vitamins allow energy to be released in the body from the food we eat every day.

Each vitamin is made up of individual chemicals which give it it's particular properties. The letters denoting each vitamin represent the order in which they were discovered. Vitamin A was the first to be discovered in 1911.

There are thirteen major vitamins and these can be divided into two major groups - those which dissolve in water, and those which dissolve in fat. The water soluble vitamins are all of the B and C group. They dissolve in water, are easily lost in cooking and cannot be stored in the body. As a result, foods containing vitamins B and C, must be eaten on a regular daily basis to ensure the body has a constant supply. Any which are additional to the body's requirements are simply excreted in the urine.

The fat soluble vitamins are A, D, E & K. These are stored in the liver, so that a daily intake is not essential. A good quantity of a rich sources, eaten once a week, is usually sufficient. Fat soluble vitamins are generally stable, but they can be sensitive to light. Freezing, however, does little damage to most.

Varying requirements

The amount of any vitamin required each day varies

according to age, sex, and occupation. Growing children and pregnant and breast feeding mothers, all need more vitamins, along with the elderly and those recovering from illness. Other factors, such as diet and lifestyle also influence vitamin requirements. The chemicals contained in alcohol, cigarettes, coffee, aspirins and the Pill use up much of the body's resources. So people who smoke, drink or take regular medication need to be sure that their food is rich in vitamins.

Is there any chance of not getting enough vitamins?

Clinical deficiencies in the West today are very rare. Marginal deficiencies however may lead to non specific symptoms such as; generally feeling unwell, a low resistance to infections, and possible restricted growth in children. The good news is that, with very few exceptions, eating a well balanced diet with sufficient variety and quantity, should provide the correct daily requirement.

Storing, preparing and cooking fruit and vegetables

Fruit and vegetables are a particularly good source of vitamins, but to obtain maximum benefit, they must be treated with care.

Firstly, look out for the freshest fruit and vegetables you can find - if possible, grow you own. Fresh produce is best eaten within a few days of purchase, since the vitamin content falls daily, especially if they are stored at room temperature. The refrigerator helps reduce the rate of calcium lost. However, if the fruit or vegetables are not required for a few days, blanch and freeze for maximum vitamin value. It's interesting to know that frozen vegetables retain many more vitamins than the tinned varieties.

Where possible eat fruit and vegetables with the skin on. Peel only when you absolutely have to. Brush the skins instead of scraping them too, since there's a wealth of nutrients in the skin.

Avoid soaking vegetables in water for long periods of time before cooking, as this causes the water soluble vitamins to leach out into the water and be lost.

Ensure that vegetables are boiled in the minimum amount of water, for a minimum amount of time, to reduce vitamin loss. Use vegetable cooking water in stocks or soups. Steaming is an effective way of cooking vegetables, since they do not come into direct contact with the water. However, steaming may take a few minutes longer than boiling.

Microwaving fruit and vegetables is an excellent cooking method. The cooking time is short, and a minimum amount of liquid is used, so the loss of vitamins is minimised.

Make sure you serve raw or cooked vegetables as soon as possible after preparation.

Counting the calories

A surprising number of the population is overweight, so it is hardly surprising that dieting is so common. Most dieters crave quick results, but is this the answer?

All about calories

We have all heard the term calories in relation to slimming, but what exactly are they?

The food we eat supplies us with the energy we need to function. Much of this energy is used up in vital body functions, such as keeping the heart beating, the lungs breathing and sustaining the other vital operations that keep the body running. Of course energy is also needed for daily activities, such as walking, talking, eating etc.

Surprisingly, 75% of the energy provided by food is used as heat for the body, and 25% is converted into 'work'.

Calories therefore, provide a useful unit to measure the potential energy content of any food, as well as the amount of energy consumed during any physical activity.

Which foods provide the most calories?

Fat, carbohydrate and protein provide the body with calories. Fat is more than twice as high in calories than either carbohydrate or protein.

Cooking oil, for example is 100% carbohydrate. Most foods, however, are a combination of different components.

Wholemeal bread is not only a good source of calories, but it also provides fibre, vitamins and other nutrients, and so is an ideal energy-giving food.

How many calories do we need?

The amount of energy consumed, and therefore the amount of calories needed, depends on age, sex and the level of activity. Obviously the more active you are, the more energy you will require.

Getting the balance right

If you take in more calories than you use, the excess is stored as body fat. If you take in less, you will lose weight, the body will start to use up fat stores.

Advantages of exercise

There are several important reasons why you should exercise when slimming:

• It makes you more aware of your body

• It increases body heat, speeding up the rate at which calories are burnt. It can also discourage eating for a few hours

• It tones muscles, and good muscle tone can do much to improve the body shape

• It enhances the self image and self confidence, so comfort eating is less appealing

Which diet?

There are so many different types of diet; from low fat, high fibre, high protein, low carbohydrate to fat-free diets.
The success of any diet (in terms of weight loss) relies on the principle that less calories should be eaten than used.
However, many people opt for crash diets where you may lose weight quickly over a short period of time, but as soon as you stop, the weight tends to creep on again. Therefore, crash dieting is never really any use, since it is only maintained for a short time.
Then there's the calorie controlled diet. Whilst following a reduced eating plan, it is very important to eat the right foods. When calorie counting alone, it is all too easy to sue the allowance on 'foods' which are in fact

'empty calories' i.e. foods with no additional nutritional value such as alcohol. Instead, you should be aiming to take in as many different nutrients as possible from a wide selection of unrefined foods.

How to eat less calories and still maintain weight

The successful diet is one that maintains a healthy eating plan. This should be one where you don't feel too deprived, something that can become a good eating pattern for life. You should retrain yourself to eat 3 sensible meals a day which are high in fibre, low in fat and sugar and teach yourself not to nibble between meals. So at the end of a successful diet, you should not be reaching for the chocolate biscuits - in fact you should not think in terms of an end. During the diet you will hopefully not only have reshaped your figure, but also your eating habits.
The low calorie recipes in this book provide tempting yet imaginative ideas to help you provide a variety of tasty dishes that are good for your waistline too.

Using this book for a life long healthy eating plan

So in conclusion, the message is loud and clear. To maintain a healthy lifestyle eat less fat, particularly saturated fat, less sugar, less salt and more whole, fresh, fibre-rich cereals, fruit and vegetables. We should possibly learn to change the emphasis of our meals. The foods of animal

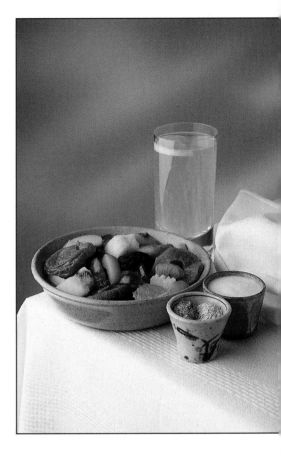

Healthy breakfasts can be tasty as well as low in calories.

origin should be eaten sparingly, and served as an accompaniment to a lavish selection of foods of vegetable origin.
The key to successfully fulfilling this plan is to eat a wide variety of foods. Packed full of deliciously healthy recipes, this book will ensure you'll never be stuck for choice.
There's no need to limit yourself to using just one or two sections of the book as they are all interchangeable. So have fun creating imaginative mix and match menus from the sugar-free, low salt, low cholesterol, vitamin rich and low caloric recipes, to ensure that you provide irresistibly tasty food which is reassuringly good for you.

LOW
CHOLESTEROL

Introduction

Health and diet are inextricably linked to such a degree that none of us can afford to regard healthy eating simply as a fad. Heart disease in particular, is one of the most common fatal conditions in the Western world, and one of the most crucial factors which causes this is a high cholesterol diet.

Cholesterol is a fatty substance found in all animal tissue and it is also produced in the body by the liver. Essentially, cholesterol is needed to carry fats through the bloodstream. Problems occur when too much fat builds up and is left on the walls of arteries, narrowing them and restricting the blood flow around the body. If this flow becomes completely blocked, a heart attack will occur.

In order to reduce excess cholesterol we must change our eating habits by reducing the amount of animal tissue and animal fat which we eat.

Research has shown that by eating non-animal fats the blood levels of cholesterol can actually be reduced. The reason being that vegetable fats are mainly polyunsaturated and these help to regulate the blood flow and keep the arteries clear of fatty deposits. Polyunsaturated fats from vegetables can therefore be included freely in a low cholesterol diet but high fat animal products such as red meat, pork and dairy foods must be restricted. Fish contains a type of fat called mono-unsaturated, which has no effect on cholesterol levels and can therefore be included in your diet without any detrimental effect. Shellfish, however, are very high in cholesterol and should be avoided completely.

One point to watch out for is that some products, such as margarines, are not always as 'healthy' as their packaging suggests. A production method called hydrogenation actually changes polyunsaturated fats into saturates, so look on labels and do not buy items which contain 'hydrogenated vegetable oils' or 'hydrogenated unsaturated fats.'

These low cholesterol recipes have been developed to offer a wide choice of favourite items which combine healthy eating with flavour and variety. So delve inside and you will realise that as well as protecting your health, nutritious food can also tickle your taste buds.

SERVES 4-6

ONION SOUP

This delicious recipe demonstrates that food which is good for your heart need be neither bland nor boring.

60g/2oz polyunsaturated margarine
900g/2lbs onions, peeled and thinly sliced
10ml/2 tsps sugar
60g/2oz plain flour
1.7 lts/3 pints chicken stock or water
Salt and freshly ground black pepper
5ml/1 tsp dried thyme
140ml/¼ pint dry white wine or dry sherry
12 x 2.5cm/1-inch slices French bread
30ml/2 tbsps olive oil
30g/1oz grated Cheddar cheese, optional
Fresh parsley for garnish

1. Melt the margarine in a large saucepan. Stir in the onions and add the sugar. Cook uncovered over a low heat, stirring occasionally, for 15-20 minutes or until the onions become golden brown.

2. Stir the flour into the onions and cook for 1 minute.

3. Gradually pour the stock into the onions, mixing well with each addition to blend smoothly.

4. Season with the salt, pepper and thyme, and add the wine or sherry. Return the soup to a low heat and bring to the boil.

5. Partially cover the saucepan, then simmer the soup for 20-30 minutes.

6. Brush each side of the slices of bread lightly with the olive oil and arrange them on a metal rack in a grill pan.

7. Lightly toast one side of the bread under a hot grill until it turns pale gold.

Step 1 Brown the onions in a large saucepan with the margarine and sugar.

Step 6 Lightly brush the slices of bread with the olive oil.

8. Turn the slices of bread over and sprinkle with the grated cheese, if used.

9. Return the slices of bread to the grill and cook until the cheese has melted and is golden brown, or if the cheese is not being used, until the other side of the bread has been lightly toasted.

10. Serve the soup in individual bowls with 2 or 3 of the croutons floating on the top. Garnish with fresh parsley.

Cook's Notes

Time
Preparation takes about 20 minutes, cooking takes about 45 minutes-1 hour.

Freezing
This soup freezes very well, but the croutons should be prepared fresh each time.

Cook's Tip
The addition of sugar will help the onion to brown. For a paler soup, omit the sugar and gently fry the onions until they are just soft and not browned.

Fat Type
Chicken stock contains fairly small amounts of saturated fat. The cheese contains a higher amount, but is used in such small quantities that this should not matter. Use vegetable stock and omit the cheese if desired.

SERVES 4

CELERY AND APPLE SOUP

This interesting combination of flavours produces a tasty soup that is also suitable for vegetarians.

30g/1oz polyunsaturated margarine
1 large onion, peeled and finely chopped
3 cooking apples, peeled, cored and sliced
1.2 lts/2 pints vegetable stock
1 bay leaf
Salt and freshly ground black pepper
3 sticks of celery, finely chopped
Finely sliced celery for garnish

celery. Bring to the boil, then cover and simmer for 30 minutes.

5. Using a liquidiser or food processor, blend the onion and apple mixture until it is smooth.

6. Whisk the puréed onion and apple mixture into the pan containing the stock and celery.

7. Return the pan to the heat and bring back to the boil. Garnish with the celery sticks and serve immediately

Step 2 Gently cook the apples with the onion until it begins to soften.

Step 4 Cook the celery in half of the stock, simmering until it is tender.

1. Melt the margarine in a large pan and stir in the onions. Fry gently for 5 minutes, or until the onions are soft but not browned.

2. Add the apple to the onion mixture and cook for a further 3 minutes, or until the apple begins to soften.

3. Stir half the stock into the onion and apple, along with the bay leaf and seasoning. Bring the mixture to the boil, cover and simmer for half an hour. Remove the bay leaf.

4. Put the remaining stock into another pan along with the

Step 6 Whisk the puréed onion and apples into the stock and celery, mixing well to blend evenly.

Cook's Notes

Time
Preparation takes about 15 minutes, cooking takes about 45 minutes.

Serving Idea
Serve with wholemeal rolls or a French stick.

Freezing
This recipe freezes well.

Fat Type
This recipe contains no saturated fat at all.

SERVES 6

MINESTRONE SOUP

There are numerous different recipes for minestrone. This one is high in fibre, which helps to reduce cholesterol levels in the blood, and it has hardly any saturated fats at all.

120g/4oz dried white cannellini beans
1.2 lts/2 pints vegetable stock
30ml/2 tbsps olive oil
1 large onion, peeled and finely chopped
1 clove garlic, crushed
1 stick celery, thinly sliced
2 carrots, peeled and diced
120g/4oz spring greens, finely shredded
60g/2oz cut green beans
1 large courgette, trimmed and diced
120g/4oz tomatoes, peeled, seeded and diced
1 bay leaf
60g/2oz wholemeal pasta
15ml/1 tbsp fresh chopped basil
15ml/1 tbsp fresh chopped parsley
Salt and freshly ground black pepper

1. Put the beans into a large bowl and cover with the vegetable stock. Leave to soak overnight. During this time the beans will double in volume.

2. Heat the oil in a large saucepan and gently fry the onion and garlic until they have softened, but not browned.

3. Stir in the celery, carrots, spring greens, green beans and courgettes. Fry gently, stirring until they have just began to soften.

4. Add the beans with the stock to the pan of vegetables, along with the tomatoes, bay leaf, pasta and seasoning. Bring to the boil, then cover and simmer for about 1 hour, or until the beans are very tender. Stir occasionally during this time to prevent the ingredients from sticking.

5. Stir in the basil and parsley, heat through for 5 minutes and serve immediately.

Step 1 Soak the beans overnight in the vegetable stock. They will double in volume during this time.

Step 4 Add the beans and stock to the partially cooked vegetables.

Cook's Notes

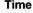

Time
Preparation takes about 20 minutes, plus overnight soaking for the beans. Cooking takes about 1½ hours.

Serving Idea
Serve with crusty wholemeal rolls.

Watchpoint
It is most important to cook any dried beans very thoroughly as they can be dangerous if eaten before they are sufficiently cooked.

Variation
Use red kidney beans instead of the white cannellini beans in this recipe.

Fat Type
Olive oil contains polyunsaturated fat and the pasta contains negligible amounts of saturated fat.

SERVES 4

VICHYSSOISE

Although this French soup is usually eaten cold, it also delicious served hot.

3 large leeks
30g/1oz polyunsaturated margarine
1 medium-sized onion, peeled and sliced
2 medium-sized potatoes, peeled and thinly sliced
570ml/1 pint vegetable stock
Salt and ground white pepper
280ml/½ pint skimmed milk
Finely chopped parsley or chives, for garnish

1. Trim the top and bottom from the leeks and peel away the outer leaf.

2. Slit the leeks lengthways down one side cutting right into the centre of the vegetable.

3. Hold the leek under running cold water, allowing it to wash any bits of soil or grit from in between the leaves.

4. Slice the leeks very thinly using a sharp knife.

5. Melt the margarine in a saucepan and add the leek and sliced onion. Cover and allow to sweat gently over a low heat for about 10 minutes.

6. Add the potatoes to the leek mixture, and pour in the stock.

7. Season with the salt and pepper, cover and cook gently for 15 minutes, or until the potatoes are soft.

8. Using a liquidiser or food processor, purée the soup until it is smooth.

9. Return the puréed soup to the saucepan and stir in the milk. Adjust the seasoning and reheat very gently until it is almost boiling. Remove from heat.

10. Either serve the soup immediately or allow to cool, then chill in a refrigerator for at least 2 hours.

Step 2 Slit the leeks lengthways down one side, cutting into the centre of each vegetable.

Step 3 Hold the slit leeks under cold running water, allowing it to penetrate between the leaves to wash out any soil or grit.

Step 8 Purée the leek and potato mixture in a liquidiser or food processor, until it is very smooth.

11. Serve garnished with the finely chopped parsley or chives.

Cook's Notes

Time
Preparation takes about 15 minutes, plus chilling time.
Cooking takes about 30 minutes.

Serving Idea
Serve with lightly toasted slices of wholemeal bread.

Freezing
This soup freezes very well.

Fat Type
This soup contains a minimal amount of saturated fat in the milk.

SERVES 4

CHICKEN SATAY

This typical Indonesian dish is very spicy, but uses ingredients which are all low in fat, making it an excellent appetizer for four.

30ml/2 tbsps soy sauce
30ml/2 tbsps sesame oil
30ml/2 tbsps lime juice
5ml/1 tsp ground cumin
5ml/1 tsp turmeric powder
10ml/2 tsps ground coriander
450g/1lb chicken breast, cut into 2.5cm/1-inch cubes
30ml/2 tbsps peanut oil
1 small onion, very finely chopped or minced
5ml/1 tsp chilli powder
120g/4oz crunchy peanut butter
5ml/1 tsp brown sugar
Lime wedges and coriander leaves, for garnish

1. Put the soy sauce, sesame oil, lime juice, cumin, turmeric and coriander into a large bowl and mix well.

2. Add the cubed chicken to the soy sauce marinade and stir well to coat the meat evenly.

3. Cover with cling film or a damp cloth and allow to stand in a refrigerator for at least 1 hour, but preferably overnight.

4. Drain the meat, reserving the marinade.

5. Thread the meat onto 4 large or 8 small skewers and set aside.

6. Heat the peanut oil in a small saucepan and add the onion and chilli powder. Cook gently until the onion is slightly softened.

7. Stir the reserved marinade into the oil and onion mixture, along with the peanut butter and brown sugar. Heat gently, stirring constantly, until all the ingredients are well blended.

Step 5 Thread the marinated meat onto 4 large, or 8 small, kebab skewers.

Step 9 Brush the partially grilled chicken with a little of the peanut sauce to baste.

8. If the sauce is too thick, stir in 2-4 tbsps boiling water.

9. Arrange the skewers of meat on a grill pan and cook under a preheated moderate grill for 10-15 minutes. After the first 5 minutes of cooking, brush the skewered meat with a little of the peanut sauce to baste.

10. During the cooking time turn the meat frequently to cook it on all sides and prevent it browning.

11. Serve the skewered meat garnished with the lime and coriander leaves, and the remaining sauce separately.

Cook's Notes

Time
Preparation takes about 25 minutes, cooking takes about 15 minutes.

Serving Idea
Serve with a mixed salad.

Variation
Use a selection of fresh vegetables instead of the chicken to make a vegetarian alternative, which would contain no saturated fat at all.

Fat Type
Chicken contains low amounts of saturated fat. The remaining ingredients contain unsaturated fats.

SERVES 4-6

SPICY VEGETABLE FRITTERS WITH TOMATO SAUCE

This delicious dish makes a ideal starter or interesting snack. Use any favourite vegetables or those that are in season.

120g/4oz plain flour
120g/4oz wholemeal flour
5ml/1 tsp salt
5ml/1 tsp chilli powder
5ml/1 tsp ground cumin
280ml/½ pint water
15ml/1 tbsp lemon juice
1 small cauliflower, broken into small florets
1 aubergine, cut into 2.5cm/1-inch cubes
3 courgettes, trimmed and cut into 2.5cm/1-inch pieces
225g/8oz button mushrooms
1 red pepper, seeded and cut into 5mm/¼-inch thick
    rounds
1 green pepper, seeded and cut into 5mm/¼-inch thick
    rounds
1 large potato, peeled and cut into 2.5cm/1-inch cubes
400g/14oz canned plum tomatoes, drained
1 red chilli, seeded and chopped
1 clove garlic, crushed
1 small onion, peeled and finely chopped
15ml/1 tbsp white wine vinegar
15ml/1 tbsp soft brown sugar
Salt the freshly ground black pepper, to taste
1 sliced green chilli for garnish
1 sliced red chilli for garnish

1. Put the flours, salt, chilli powder and cumin into a large bowl. Make a slight well in the centre.

2. Gradually add the water and lemon juice to the flour, beating well until a smooth batter is formed.

3. Wash the fresh vegetables and allow them to drain completely on kitchen paper or a clean cloth.

4. Put the tomatoes, fresh chilli, garlic, onions, vinegar and sugar into a food processor or liquidiser and blend until the sauce is smooth.

5. Pour the sauce mixture into a small pan and heat gently, stirring until it is completely warmed through. Season with salt and transfer to a small serving dish and garnish with slices of red and green chillies.

6. Heat some vegetable oil in a deep fat fryer until it is warm enough to brown a 2.5cm/1-inch cube of bread in just under 1 minute.

7. Make sure the vegetables are completely dry, patting any moisture off them with kitchen paper if necessary.

8. Using a slotted spoon drop the vegetables, a few at a time, into the batter and dip them to coat thoroughly.

9. Remove the vegetables from the batter, again using the slotted spoon, and allow some of the batter to drain back into the bowl.

10. Drop the vegetables into the hot oil, and fry quickly until they are golden brown and the batter puffy.

11. Remove the fried vegetables from the oil and drain completely on kitchen paper, keeping them warm until all the remaining vegetables have been prepared in this manner.

12. Serve immediately, providing small forks with which to dip the vegetables into the spicy tomato sauce.

Cook's Notes

Time
Preparation takes about 20 minutes, cooking takes about ½ hour.

Watchpoint
It is important to ensure that the vegetables are completely dry before coating with the batter, or it will not cover them.

Fat Type
There is no saturated fat in this dish, but it is important to check that the oil used in the deep fat frying is polyunsaturated and that it is fresh.

SERVES 6

TUNA, BEAN AND TOMATO SALAD

Fish is of great value in a low cholesterol diet as it contains mono-unsaturated fats which do not affect the cholesterol level in the blood.

225g/8oz dried flageolet beans
180g/6oz canned tuna in brine
Juice of 1 lemon
140ml/¼ pint olive oil
5ml/1 tsp chopped fresh herbs, e.g. parsley, basil or
  marjoram
Salt and freshly ground black pepper
8 firm tomatoes

1. Put the beans into a bowl and pour over enough cold water to just cover. Allow to soak overnight.

2. Drain the beans and put them into a saucepan. Cover with boiling water, then simmer for at least 1 hour. Drain thoroughly and cool.

3. Drain the can of tuna and flake it into a bowl.

4. Put the lemon juice, olive oil, herbs and seasoning into a small bowl and whisk together with a fork.

5. Stir the beans into the tuna fish and mix in the dressing, tossing the salad together carefully so that the tuna does not break up too much, but the dressing is thoroughly incorporated.

6. Adjust the seasoning and arrange the salad in a mound on a shallow serving dish.

7. Cut a small cross into the skins of the tomato and plunge them into boiling water for 30 seconds.

8. Using a sharp knife carefully peel away the skins from the tomatoes.

9. Slice the tomatoes thinly and arrange them around the edge of the bean and tuna salad. Serve immediately.

Step 5 Mix the dressing into the salad by tossing it carefully, to ensure that the tuna does not break up too much.

Step 8 When blanched, the skins on the tomatoes should peel away very easily if you use a sharp knife.

Cook's Notes

Time
Preparation takes about 25 minutes, plus overnight soaking.

Variation
Use any type of bean of your choice.

Watchpoint
Great care must be taken with cooking beans, as any that are under cooked could be dangerous when eaten.

Fat Type
This recipe contains mono-unsaturated and polyunsaturated fats.

Serving Idea
Serve with a simple lettuce salad.

SERVES 4

SMOKED MACKEREL PÂTÉ

Smoked fish has a wonderful flavour and is ideal for making pâté.

225g/8oz smoked mackerel fillets, skin and bones removed
60g/2oz polyunsaturated margarine
Juice of half an orange
5ml/1 tsp tomato purée
5ml/1 tsp white wine vinegar
Salt and freshly ground black pepper, optional
1 x 113g/3½ oz can pimento peppers, drained
280ml/½ pint clear vegetable stock
10ml/2 tsps powdered gelatin
30ml/2 tbsps dry sherry
30ml/2 tbsps cold water

1. Put the mackerel, margarine, orange juice, purée, vinegar and seasonings into a liquidiser or food processor and blend until smooth.

2. Put the pâté into a serving dish and smooth the top evenly.

3. Cut the pimentos into thin strips and arrange in a lattice over the top of the pâté.

4. Bring the stock to the boil in a small pan. Remove from the heat and cool for 1 minute.

5. Sprinkle over the gelatin and allow to stand, stirring occasionally until it has completely dissolved.

6. When the gelatin has dissolved the liquid should be

Step 3 Arrange the strips of pimento in a lattice pattern over the top of the pâté.

Step 5 Sprinkle the gelatine over the hot stock and allow it to stand, to dissolve completely.

clear. At this point stir in the sherry and cold water.

7. Very carefully spoon the aspic over the top of the mackerel pâté and the pimentos, taking great care not to dislodge the lattice pattern.

8. Chill the pâté in a refrigerator until the aspic has completely set.

Cook's Notes

 Time
Preparation takes about 30 minutes, plus chilling time.
Cooking takes about 2 minutes.

 Variation
Use any type of smoked fish in place of the mackerel in this recipe.

 Preparation
If you do not have a food processor or blender, this pâté can be made by mashing with a fork, but it will not have such a smooth texture.

 Fat Type
Fish contains mono-unsaturated fat which does not affect the cholesterol level in the blood.

 Serving Idea
Serve with crusty wholemeal bread or French toast.

SERVES 4-6

TOMATO AND PEPPER ICE

Similar to frozen gazpacho, this appetizer is ideal for serving on warm summer days. It could also be used, in smaller quantities, as a palate freshener between courses in place of a conventional sweet sorbet.

6 ice cubes
115ml/4 fl oz canned tomato juice
Juice 1 lemon
5ml/1 tsp Worcestershire sauce
½ small green pepper, seeded and roughly chopped
½ small red pepper, seeded and roughly chopped

1. Break the ice into small pieces using a small hammer.

2. Put the broken ice into a blender or food processor, along with the tomato juice, lemon juice and Worcestershire sauce. Blend the mixture until it becomes slushy.

3. Pour the tomato mixture into ice trays and freeze for ½ hour, or until it is just half frozen.

4. Using a sharp knife, chop the peppers into very small pieces.

5. Remove the tomato ice from the freezer trays and put it into a bowl.

6. Mash the tomato ice with the back of a fork until the crystals are well broken up.

7. Mix in the chopped peppers and return the tomato ice to the freezer trays.

8. Re-freeze for a further 1½ hours, stirring occasionally to prevent the mixture from solidifying completely.

9. To serve, allow the tomato ice to defrost for about 5 minutes, then mash with the back of a fork to roughly break up the ice crystals. Serve in small glass dishes which have been chilled beforehand.

Step 2 Blend the ice, tomato juice, lemon juice and Worcestershire sauce until it becomes a smooth slush.

Step 6 Mash the semi-frozen tomato ice with the back of a fork to break up the ice crystals finely.

Step 8 During the freezing time, keep stirring the tomato and pepper ice with a fork, to prevent the mixture from becoming a solid block.

Cook's Notes

Time
Preparation takes about 15 minutes, plus freezing time.

Freezing
This recipe will freeze for up to 2 months.

Watchpoint
Take care not to allow the tomato ice to freeze into a solid block, or it will be too hard to break into rough crystals.

Serving Idea
Scoop out the tomatoes and serve this ice in the shells, instead of glass dishes.

Fat Type
There is no fat in this recipe.

SERVES 4

SUMMER PASTA SALAD

Lightly cooked summer vegetables and wholemeal pasta are combined to create this delicious wholesome salad.

1 aubergine
1 courgette
1 red pepper
1 green pepper
1 medium-sized onion
2 large tomatoes
60ml/4 tbsps olive oil
1 clove garlic, crushed
Salt and freshly ground black pepper
225g/8oz wholemeal pasta spirals
15ml/1 tbsp vinegar
2.5ml/½ tsp dry English mustard

Step 1 Sprinkle the aubergine slices liberally with salt and allow them to de-gorge for 30 minutes to remove their bitterness.

1. Cut the aubergine into 1cm/½-inch slices. Sprinkle the slices liberally with salt and allow to stand for 30 minutes.

2. Using a sharp knife, trim the courgettes and cut into 6mm/¼-inch slices.

3. Cut the peppers in half and carefully remove the cores and seeds. Using a sharp knife, cut the pepper into thin strips.

4. Peel and finely chop the onion.

5. Cut a small cross in the skins of the tomatoes and plunge them into boiling water for 30 seconds. After this time remove the tomatoes and carefully peel away the skins.

6. Cut the peeled tomatoes into 8. Remove and discard the pips from each tomato slice.

7. Put 30ml/2 tbsps of the olive oil in a frying pan and stir in the onion. Fry gently until it is transparent, but not coloured.

8. Thoroughly rinse the salt from the aubergine slices and pat them dry on absorbent kitchen paper. Roughly chop the slices.

9. Add the chopped aubergine, courgette, peppers, tomatoes and garlic to the cooked onion and fry very

Step 9 Gently fry all the vegetables together, stirring frequently to prevent them from browning.

gently for 20 minutes, or until just soft. Season with salt and pepper and allow to cool.

10. Put the pasta spirals in a large saucepan and cover with boiling water. Sprinkle in a little salt and simmer for 10 minutes or until tender but still firm.

11. Rinse the pasta in cold water and drain very well.

12. Whisk together the remaining olive oil, the vinegar and mustard in a small bowl. Season with salt and pepper.

13. Put the pasta and cooled vegetables into a serving dish and pour over the dressing, tossing the ingredients together to coat them evenly. Serve well chilled.

Cook's Notes

Time
Preparation takes approximately 40 minutes, cooking takes 30 minutes.

Preparation
Make sure that the aubergine is rinsed very thoroughly or the salad will be much too salty.

Fat Type
Olive oil contains polyunsaturated fat and is therefore beneficial to those on a low cholesterol diet.

SERVES 4

MUSHROOM PASTA SALAD

*Mushrooms are always delicious in a salad and this recipe, which combines
them with wholemeal pasta shapes, is no exception.*

75ml/5 tbsps olive oil
Juice of 2 lemons
5ml/1 tsp fresh chopped basil
5ml/1 tsp fresh chopped parsley
Salt and freshly ground black pepper
225g/8oz mushrooms
225g/8oz wholemeal pasta shapes of your choice

boiling water. Season with a little salt and simmer for 10 minutes, or until just tender.

5. Rinse the pasta in cold water and drain well.

6. Add the pasta to the marinated mushrooms and lemon dressing, mixing well to coat evenly.

7. Adjust the seasoning if necessary, then chill well before serving.

Step 1 Whisk the lemon juice, herbs and seasoning together in a large bowl using a fork.

Step 2 Use a sharp knife to slice the mushrooms thinly.

1. In a large bowl mix together the olive oil, lemon juice, herbs and seasoning.

2. Finely slice the mushrooms and add these to the lemon dressing in the bowl, stirring well to coat the mushrooms evenly.

3. Cover the bowl with cling film and allow to stand in a cool place for at least 1 hour.

4. Put the pasta into a large saucepan and cover with

Step 6 Stir the cooled pasta into the marinated mushrooms, mixing well to coat evenly.

Cook's Notes

Time
Preparation takes approximately 10 minutes, plus 1 hour at least for the mushrooms to marinate. Cooking takes about 15 minutes.

Variation
Use a mixture of button and wild mushrooms for a delicious variation in flavour.

Serving Idea
Serve mushroom pasta salad on a bed of mixed lettuce.

Fat Type
Olive oil contains polyunsaturated fat and is beneficial for those on a low cholesterol diet.

SERVES 4-6

STIR-FRY TOFU SALAD

Ideal for vegetarians, but so delicious that it will be enjoyed by everyone.

1 cake of tofu
120g/4oz mange tout
60g/2oz mushrooms
2 carrots, peeled
2 sticks celery
60g/2oz broccoli florets
140ml/¼ pint vegetable oil
45ml/3 tbsps lemon juice
10ml/2 tsps honey
5ml/1 tsp grated fresh ginger
45ml/3 tbsps soy sauce
Dash of sesame oil
4 spring onions
60g/2oz unsalted roasted peanuts
120g/4oz bean sprouts
½ head Chinese leaves

1. Drain the tofu well and press gently to remove any excess moisture. Cut into 1.25cm/½-inch cubes.

2. Trim the tops and tails from the mange tout peas.

3. Thinly slice the mushrooms with a sharp knife.

4. Cut the carrots and celery into thin slices, angling your knife so that each slice is cut on the diagonal.

5. Trim the spring onions and slice them in the same way as the carrots and celery.

6. Heat 30ml/2 tbsps of the vegetable oil in a wok or large frying pan. Stir in the mange tout, mushrooms, celery, carrots and broccoli, and cook for 2 minutes, stirring constantly.

7. Remove the vegetables from the wok and set them aside to cool.

8. Put the remaining oil into a small bowl and whisk in the lemon juice, honey, ginger, soy sauce and sesame oil.

9. Stir the sliced spring onions, peanuts and bean sprouts into the cooled vegetables.

10. Mix the dressing into the salad vegetables, then add the tofu. Toss the tofu into the salad very carefully so that it does not break up.

11. Shred the Chinese leaves and arrange them on a serving platter. Pile the salad ingredients over the top and serve well chilled.

Step 4 Slice the carrots and celery thinly, cutting with your knife at an angle to produce diagonal pieces

Step 10 Toss the tofu very carefully into the salad ingredients taking care not the break it up.

Cook's Notes

Time
Preparation takes approximately 25 minutes, cooking takes 2-4 minutes.

Preparation
Make sure that the stir-fried vegetables are completely cool before adding the remaining salad ingredients, or they will lose their crispness.

Variation
Shredded cooked chicken can be used in place of the tofu in this recipe.

Fat Type
All the fat in this recipe is polyunsaturated.

SERVES 6-8

MIXED PEPPER SALAD

It is now possible to buy sweet peppers in a variety of colours, so include as many as you wish in this eye-catching salad.

3 red peppers
3 green peppers
3 yellow peppers
30ml/2 tbsps vegetable oil
90ml/6 tbsps sunflower oil
30ml/2 tbsps lemon juice
30ml/2 tbsps white wine vinegar
1 small clove garlic, crushed
Pinch salt
Pinch cayenne pepper
Pinch sugar
3 hard-boiled eggs
60g/2oz black olives, stoned
30ml/2 tbsps finely chopped fresh coriander leaves,
     optional

Step 2 Put the cored pepper halves cut side down on a flat surface and gently press them with the palm of your hand to flatten them out.

1. Cut all the peppers in half and remove the seeds and cores.

2. With the palm of your hand lightly press the halved peppers down onto a flat surface, to flatten them out.

3. Brush the skin side of each pepper with a little of the vegetable oil and place under a preheated hot grill.

4. Cook until the skins begin to char and split.

5. Remove the peppers from the grill and wrap them in a clean tea towel. Allow to stand for 10-15 minutes.

6. Put the sunflower oil, lemon juice, vinegar, garlic, salt, pepper and sugar into a small bowl and whisk together well.

7. Shell the eggs and cut each one into four.

Step 4 Cook the oiled peppers under the grill until the skin begins to char and split.

8. Unwrap the peppers and carefully peel away the burnt skin. Cut the pepper flesh into thick strips about 2.5cm/1-inch wide.

9. Arrange the pepper strips in a circle alternating the colours all the way round.

10. Arrange the olives and quartered eggs in the centre.

11. Sprinkle with the coriander leaves, and spoon over all the dressing.

12. Chill the salad for at least 1 hour before serving.

Cook's Notes

 Time
Preparation takes 20 minutes, cooking takes about 5 minutes.

 Serving Idea
Serve this salad with crusty French bread or rolls.

 Cook's Tip
Peeled peppers will keep in a refrigerator for up to 5 days if they are covered with a little oil.

 Fat Type
This recipe is high in polyunsaturated fats. The eggs contain saturated fats, but can be omitted if desired.

SERVES 4

CHEESY STUFFED TOMATOES

Although cheese should be avoided on a low fat diet, soft cheeses such as Brie and Camembert do have a lower fat content than Cheddar and in small amounts can provide welcome variety in a restricted diet.

4 beefsteak tomatoes
4 anchovy fillets
15g/½oz capers, drained
2 spring onions
120g/4oz Camembert or Brie cheese, rind removed
10ml/2 tsps caraway seeds
Salt and freshly ground black pepper
Lettuce to garnish

1. Cut a slice from the rounded end of each tomato and carefully scoop out the pulp and seeds. Strain out the seeds and reserve the pulp and juice for the filling.

Step 1 Strain the seeds out of the tomato pulp, keeping only the pulp and juice for use in the recipe.

2. Put the anchovies in a bowl and cover with a little milk. Allow to soak for 5 minutes to remove the saltiness.

3. Drain and rinse the anchovies, then pat them dry. Chop the anchovies finely.

4. Put the capers and spring onions onto a board and chop them finely also.

5. Put the cheese into a bowl and mash it with a fork.

6. Stir in the capers, anchovies, onions, caraway seeds, tomato juice and pulp. Mix together thoroughly, then season with a little salt and pepper.

7. Carefully spoon the cheese filling into the hollowed out tomatoes and arrange them on a serving plate.

Step 7 Carefully pile the cheese filling back into the hollowed out tomatoes.

8. Replace the sliced tops and serve them well chilled on a bed of lettuce.

Cook's Notes

 Time
Preparation takes 15 minutes, plus chilling time of at least 1 hour.

Preparation
Use a grapefruit knife or serrated teaspoon to remove the centres of the tomatoes.

 Variation
Use cottage or curd cheese instead of the Camembert or Brie.

 Serving Idea
Serve with a vinaigrette dressing and wholemeal bread or rolls.

 Fat Type
The cheese contains saturated fat, so should only be eaten in moderation.

SERVES 4

MEDITERRANEAN AUBERGINES

These delicious stuffed aubergines can be served as an accompaniment to a main meal for four or as a lunch dish for two.

2 small aubergines
30g/1oz polyunsaturated margarine
1 small onion, finely chopped
1 clove garlic, crushed
120g/4oz tomatoes
150g/5oz long grain rice, cooked
10ml/2 tsps fresh chopped marjoram
Pinch cinnamon
Salt and freshly ground black pepper

1. Preheat an oven to 180°C/350°F/Gas Mark 4. Wrap the aubergines in aluminium foil and bake for 20 minutes to soften. Allow to cool.

2. Cut the aubergines in half, then using a serrated teaspoon or grapefruit knife, carefully scoop out the pulp leaving a 1.25cm/½-inch border to form a shell.

3. Melt the margarine in a frying pan and gently sauté the onion and garlic until they are just soft.

4. Chop the aubergine pulp roughly and stir into the pan along with the onions. Cover and cook for about 5 minutes.

5. Cut a small cross in the skins of the tomatoes and plunge them into boiling water for 30 seconds.

6. Remove the tomatoes from the water and carefully peel away the skin using a sharp knife.

7. Quarter the tomatoes and remove and discard the pips. Chop the tomato flesh roughly and stir into the cooked aubergine and onion mixture, along with the rice, marjoram and cinnamon. Season with salt and pepper.

8. Carefully pile the rice filling back into the aubergine shells and arrange them on an ovenproof dish or baking tray. Cover with aluminium foil.

9. Return to the oven and bake for 20 minutes. Serve hot, garnished with a little finely chopped parsley if desired.

Step 2 Carefully scoop the pulp out of each eggplant half with a serrated spoon or grapefruit knife, leaving a thin border on the inside to form a shell.

Step 7 Remove and discard the seeds from the peeled tomatoes.

Cook's Notes

 Time
Preparation takes 25 minutes, cooking takes about 40 minutes.

 Preparation
Take care not to split the aubergine shells when scooping out the pulp.

 Variation
60g/2oz mature Cheddar cheese can be added to the filling if desired or allowed!

 Fat Type
This recipe contains only polyunsaturated fats.

SERVES 4

Chicken with 'Burnt' Peppers and Coriander

'Burning' peppers is a technique for removing the skins which also imparts a delicious flavour to this favourite vegetable.

2 red peppers, halved and seeded
1 green pepper, halved and seeded
60ml/4 tbsps vegetable oil, for brushing
15ml/1 tbsp olive oil
10ml/2 tsps paprika
1.25ml/¼ tsp ground cumin
Pinch cayenne pepper
2 cloves garlic, crushed
450g/1lb canned tomatoes, drained and chopped
45ml/3 tbsps fresh chopped coriander
45ml/3 tbsps fresh chopped parsley
Salt, for seasoning
4 large chicken breasts, boned
1 large onion, sliced
60g/2oz flaked almonds

1. Put the peppers, cut side down, on a flat surface and gently press them with the palm of your hand to flatten them out.

2. Brush the skin side with 30ml/2 tbsps of the vegetable oil and cook them under a hot grill until the skin chars and splits.

3. Wrap the peppers in a clean towel for 10 minutes to cool.

4. Unwrap the peppers and carefully peel off the charred skin. Chop the pepper flesh into thin strips.

5. Heat the olive oil in a frying pan and gently fry the paprika, cumin, cayenne pepper and garlic for 2 minutes, stirring to prevent the garlic from browning.

6. Stir in the tomatoes, coriander, parsley and season with a little salt. Simmer for 15-20 minutes, or until thick. Set aside.

7. Heat the remaining vegetable oil in an ovenproof dish, and sauté the chicken breasts, turning them frequently until they are golden brown on both sides.

8. Remove the chicken and set aside. Gently fry the onions in the oil for about 5 minutes, or until softened but not overcooked.

9. Return the chicken to the casserole with the onions and pour on about 280ml/½ pint of water. Bring to the boil.

10. Cover the casserole and simmer for about 30 minutes, turning the chicken occasionally to prevent it from burning.

11. Remove the chicken from the casserole and boil the remaining liquid rapidly to reduce to about 90ml/3 fl oz of stock.

12. Add the peppers and the tomato sauce to the chicken stock and stir well.

13. Return the chicken to the casserole, cover and simmer very gently for a further 30 minutes, or until the chicken is tender.

14. Arrange the chicken on a serving dish with a little of the sauce spooned over. Sprinkle with flaked almonds and serve any remaining sauce separately.

Cook's Notes

Time
Preparation takes 30 minutes, cooking takes about 1 hour 30 minutes.

Preparation
Take care not to cook this dish too rapidly or the peppers will disintegrate.

Fat Type
The chicken contains saturated fats, but only in small quantities, the rest of the dish contains only polyunsaturated fat.

SERVES 4

HERRINGS WITH APPLES

The addition of fresh tasting apples beautifully complements the delicious and wholesome flavour of herring.

4 herrings, cleaned
2 large dessert apples
1 large onion
4 large potatoes, peeled and sliced
Salt and freshly ground black pepper
140ml/¼ pint dry cider
60g/2oz dried breadcrumbs
60g/2oz polyunsaturated margarine
15ml/1 tbsp fresh chopped parsley

1. Cut the heads and tails from the herrings and split them open from the underside.

2. Put the herrings, belly side down, on a flat surface and carefully press along the back of each fish with the palm of your hand, pushing the backbone down towards the surface.

3. Turn the herrings over and with a sharp knife, carefully prise away the backbone, pulling out any loose bones as you go. Do not cut the fish into separate fillets. Wash and dry them well.

4. Peel, quarter, core and slice one of the apples. Peel and slice the onion thinly.

5. Lightly grease a shallow baking dish and layer with the potatoes, apple and onions, seasoning well with salt and pepper between layers.

6. Pour the cider over the potato layers and cover the dish with foil. Bake in a preheated oven 180°C/350°F/Gas Mark 4 for 40 minutes.

7. Remove the dish from the oven and arrange the herring fillets over the top.

8. Sprinkle the breadcrumbs over the herrings and dot

Step 2 Press down the backbone of the herrings with the palm of your hand, pushing the spine towards the work surface as you go.

Step 3 Carefully lift the backbone away from the fish with a sharp knife, pulling any loose bones out at the same time. Do not cut the fish into separate fillets.

with half of the margarine.

9. Increase the oven temperature to 200°C/400°F/Gas Mark 6 and return the dish to the oven for about 10–15 minutes, or until the herrings are cooked and brown.

10. Core the remaining apples and slice into rounds, leaving the peel on.

11. Melt the remaining margarine in a frying pan and gently fry the apple slices.

12. Remove the herrings from the oven and garnish with the fried apple slices and chopped parsley. Serve at once.

Cook's Notes

Time
Preparation takes 15-20 minutes, cooking takes about 50 minutes.

Variation
Use small mackerel instead of herrings in this recipe.

Serving Idea
Serve with a carrot, orange and watercress salad.

Fat Type
Fish contains mono-unsaturated fats which do not affect the cholesterol levels in the blood.

SERVES 6-8

SALMON TROUT WITH SPINACH AND WALNUT STUFFING

1 fresh whole salmon trout, weighing 1.25kg/2½lbs, cleaned
1kg/2lbs fresh spinach
1 small onion
60g/2oz polyunsaturated margarine
60g/2oz walnuts, roughly chopped
120g/4oz fresh white breadcrumbs
15ml/1 tbsp fresh chopped parsley
15ml/1 tbsp fresh chopped thyme
¼ tsp grated nutmeg
Salt and freshly ground black pepper
Juice 2 lemons
Watercress sprigs and lemon slices, to garnish

1. Carefully cut the underside of the fish from the end of the slit made when the fish was cleaned, to the tip of the tail.

2. Place the fish, belly side down, on a flat work surface, spreading the cut underside out to balance the fish more easily.

3. Using the palm of your hand press down along the backbone of the fish, pushing the spine downwards towards the work surface.

4. Turn the fish over and using a sharp knife, carefully pull the backbone away from the fish, cutting it away with scissors at the base of the head and tail.

5. Remove the backbone completely and pull out any loose bones you may find with a pair of tweezers. Lay the boned fish in the centre of a large square of lightly oiled aluminium foil and set aside.

6. Wash the spinach leaves well and tear off any coarse stalks. Put the spinach into a large saucepan and sprinkle with salt. Do not add any extra water. Cover and cook over a moderate heat for about 3 minutes.

7. Turn the spinach into a colander and drain well, pressing with the back of a wooden spoon to remove all the excess moisture.

8. Chop the cooked spinach very finely using a sharp knife.

9. Peel and chop the onion finely and fry gently in about 15ml/1 tbsp of the margarine until soft, but not coloured.

10. Stir the cooked onion into the chopped spinach along with the walnuts, breadcrumbs, herbs, nutmeg, salt, pepper and half of the lemon juice. Mix well to blend evenly.

11. Use the spinach stuffing to fill the cavity inside the trout. Push the stuffing in firmly, re-shaping the fish as you do so. Allow a little of the stuffing to show between the cut edge of the fish.

12. Seal the foil over the top of the fish, but do not wrap it too tightly.

13. Place the fish in a roasting tin and bake in a preheated oven at 180°C/350°F/Gas Mark 4 for 35 minutes.

14. Carefully unwrap the fish and transfer it to a large serving dish.

15. Using a sharp knife, peel away the skin from all exposed sides of the fish. If possible remove some skin from the underside also.

16. Whilst the fish is still hot, dot with the remaining margarine, sprinkle with the remaining lemon juice, then serve garnished with the watercress and sliced lemon.

Cook's Notes

Time
Preparation takes 35-40 minutes, cooking takes about 40 minutes.

Cook's Tip
If you feel that you cannot bone the fish yourself, ask your fishmonger to do it for you, but explain that you wish the bone to be removed from the underside of the fish.

Fat Type
Fish contains mono-unsaturated fats and the remainder of fats used in this recipe are all polyunsaturated.

SERVES 4

POUSSINS ESPAGNOLE

The olive oil in this recipe gives a wonderful flavour to the sauce without loading it with saturated fat.

4 small poussins
Salt and freshly ground black pepper
Olive oil, to brush
4 small wedges of lime or lemon
4 bay leaves
30ml/2 tbsps olive oil
1 small onion, thinly sliced
1 clove garlic, peeled and crushed
450g/1lb tomatoes
140ml/¼ pint red wine
140ml/¼ pint chicken or vegetable stock
15ml/1 tbsp tomato purée
1 green chillies, seeded and thinly sliced
1 small red pepper, seeded and cut into thin strips
1 small green pepper, seeded and cut into thin strips
30ml/2 tbsps chopped blanched almonds
15ml/1 tbsp pine kernels
12 small black olives, pitted
15ml/1 tbsp raisins

1. Rub the poussins inside and out with salt and pepper. Brush the skins with olive oil and push a wedge of lemon or lime, and a bay leaf into the centre of each one.

2. Roast the poussins, uncovered, in a preheated oven 190°C/375°F/Gas Mark 5 for 45 minutes, or until just tender.

3. Heat the 30ml/2 tbsps olive oil in a large frying pan and gently cook the onion and the garlic until they are soft, but not coloured.

4. Cut a slit into the skins of each tomato and plunge into boiling water for 30 seconds.

5. Using a sharp knife carefully peel away the skins from the blanched tomatoes.

6. Chop the tomatoes roughly. Remove and discard the seeds and cores.

7. Add the chopped tomatoes to the cooked onion and garlic, and fry gently for a further 2 minutes.

8. Add all the remaining ingredients and simmer for 10-15 minutes, or until the tomatoes have completely softened and the sauce has thickened slightly.

9. Arrange the poussins on a serving dish and spoon a little of the sauce over each one.

10. Serve hot with the remaining sauce in a separate jug.

Step 3 Fry the onion and garlic gently in the olive oil until they are soft but not coloured.

Step 5 Using a sharp knife carefully peel away the loosened skins from the blanched tomatoes.

Cook's Notes

 Time
Preparation takes 15 minutes, cooking takes about 1 hour.

 Serving Idea
Serve with rice and a mixed green salad.

 Cook's Tip
If the poussins start to get too brown during the cooking time, cover them with aluminium foil.

 Fat Type
Chicken contains only small amounts of saturated fats, and the remaining ingredients in this recipe contain only unsaturated fats.

SERVES 4
SAFFRON CHICKEN

The delicate colour and flavour of saffron enhances the taste of chicken and gives this dish a Mediterranean flavour.

1.5kg/2-3lb chicken
30ml/2 tbsps olive oil
Salt and freshly ground black pepper
1 small onion, peeled and finely chopped
1 clove garlic, crushed
10ml/2 tsps paprika pepper
8 tomatoes
300g/10oz long grain white rice
700ml/1¼ pints boiling water
Large pinch saffron strands or 1.25ml/¼ tsp ground
    saffron
180g/6oz frozen peas
30ml/2 tbsps chopped fresh parsley

Step 4 Remove the skin from the chicken joints by pulling and cutting with a sharp knife.

1. Cut the chicken into 8 pieces with a sharp knife or cook's cleaver, cutting lengthways down the breast bone and through the backbone, to halve it completely.

2. Cut the chicken halves in half again, slitting between the leg joint diagonally up and around the breast joint.

3. Finally cut each chicken quarter in half by cutting away the drumsticks from the leg thigh joint, and the wings from the breast joints.

4. Remove the skin from the chicken joints by pulling and cutting with a sharp knife.

5. Heat the oil in a large casserole dish or sauté pan, and fry the chicken, turning it frequently to brown evenly. Season with a little salt and pepper, then remove it from the pan and set aside.

6. Add the onions and garlic to the juices in the sauté pan and cook slowly until softened but not coloured.

7. Add the paprika to the onions and fry quickly for about 30 seconds to just burn.

8. Cut a small cross into the skins of the tomatoes and plunge them into boiling water.

9. Using a sharp knife peel away the loosened skin from each tomato.

10. Cut the tomatoes into quarters and remove the cores and seeds. Chop the tomato flesh finely and add this to the sauté pan with the paprika and the onions.

11. Cook for about 5-10 minutes to draw off the liquid from the tomatoes. The sauce mixture should be of a dropping consistency when this has been done.

12. Stir the rice, water and saffron into the tomato purée along with the browned chicken portions. Bring to the boil, reduce the heat to simmering, then cover the casserole tightly and cook for about 20 minutes.

13. Add the peas and the parsley to the casserole, stir well and continue cooking for a further 5-10 minutes, or until the rice is tender and all the liquids have been absorbed.

14. Serve very hot.

Cook's Notes

Time
Preparation takes about 25 minutes, cooking takes 30-35 minutes.

Watchpoint
Stir the casserole frequently after step 12 to prevent the rice from sticking.

Fat Type
Chicken contains small amounts of saturated fat, but the remainder in this recipe is polyunsaturated.

SERVES 4

CHICKEN LIVER STIR-FRY

Chicken livers are very low in fat and high in flavour. They also require very little cooking so are perfect for stir-fry recipes.

450g/1lb chicken livers
45ml/3 tbsps sesame oil
60g/2oz split blanched almonds
1 clove garlic, peeled
60g/2oz mange tout peas, trimmed
8-10 Chinese leaves, shredded
10ml/2 tsps cornflour
15ml/1 tbsp cold water
30ml/2 tbsps soy sauce
140ml/¼ pint chicken or vegetable stock

Step 1 Trim the chicken livers, cutting away any discoloured areas or bits of fat or tubes using a sharp knife.

1. Trim the chicken livers, removing any discoloured areas or fatty tubes.

2. Cut the chicken livers into even-sized pieces.

3. Heat a wok and pour in the oil. When the oil is hot, reduce the heat and stir-fry the almonds until they are pale golden brown. Remove the almonds, draining any oil back into the wok, and set them aside on absorbent kitchen paper.

Step 3 Stir-fry the almonds in the hot oil until they are a pale golden brown.

4. Add the garlic clove to the wok and cook for 1-2 minutes to flavour the oil only. Remove the clove of garlic and discard.

5. Stir the chicken livers into the flavoured oil and cook for 2-3 minutes, stirring frequently to brown evenly. Remove the chicken livers from the wok and set them aside.

6. Add the mange tout peas to the hot oil and stir-fry for 1 minute. Then stir in the Chinese leaves and cook for 1 minute further. Remove the vegetables and set aside.

Step 8 Cook the sauce in the wok, stirring all the time until it has thickened and cleared.

7. Mix together the cornflour and water, then blend in the soy sauce and stock.

8. Pour the cornflour mixture into the wok and bring to the boil, stirring until the sauce has thickened and cleared.

9. Return all other ingredients to the wok and heat through for 1 minute. Serve immediately.

Cook's Notes

Time
Preparation takes 25 minutes, cooking takes 5-6 minutes.

Variation
Use finely sliced lamb or calves' liver in place of the chicken livers.

Serving Idea
Serve with fried rice or noodles.

Fat Type
Liver contains saturated fat, but in very small quantities.

SERVES 4-6

CHICKEN WITH LEMON JULIENNE

Lean chicken served with a tangy julienne of fresh vegetables makes a delicious main course - ideal for those on a low cholesterol diet.

1 x 1.5kg/3lb chicken
30ml/2 tbsps olive oil
30ml/2 tbsps polyunsaturated margarine
2 sticks celery
2 carrots
1 small onion, peeled and thinly sliced
15ml/1 tbsp chopped fresh basil
1 bay leaf
Juice and grated rind of 2 small lemons
140ml/¼ pint water
Salt and freshly ground black pepper
Pinch sugar, optional
Lemon slices for garnish

1. Cut the chicken into 8 pieces with a sharp knife or a cook's cleaver, cutting the chicken lengthways down the breastbone and through the backbone to halve it completely.

2. Cut the chicken halves in half again, slitting between the leg joint diagonally up and around the breast joint.

3. Finally cut each chicken quarter in half by cutting away the drumsticks from the leg thigh joint, and the wings from the breast joints.

4. Remove the skin from the chicken joints by pulling and cutting with a sharp knife.

5. Heat the oil in a large sauté pan along with the margarine. Gently fry the chicken pieces, turning them frequently to brown evenly.

6. Remove the chicken pieces to a plate and set aside.

7. Using a sharp knife cut the celery into pieces 3.5cm/1½-inches long. Cut these pieces into long thin matchsticks lengthways.

8. Cut the carrots into similar length pieces, then cut each piece in half lengthways. Continue cutting each carrot half into the same sized pieces as the celery.

9. Stir the carrots and celery into the chicken juices, along with the onion. Cook over a gentle heat for about 3 minutes or until just beginning to soften but not brown.

10. Stir the basil, bay leaf, lemon juice and rind, the water, salt and pepper into the vegetables, mix well and cook for 2-3 minutes.

11. Return the chicken portions to the casserole and bring the mixture to the boil.

12. Cover the pan and reduce the heat. Allow the casserole to simmer for about 35-45 minutes, or until the chicken is tender and the juices will run clear when the meat is pierced with a sharp knife.

13. Remove the chicken and vegetables to a serving dish and discard the bay leaf.

14. Heat the sauce quickly to thicken if necessary. Adjust the flavour of the sauce with the sugar if desired.

15. Spoon the sauce over the chicken and garnish with the lemon slices.

Cook's Notes

Time
Preparation takes 40 minutes, cooking will take about 55 minutes.

Serving Idea
Serve with rice and a green salad.

Watchpoint
Make sure that the chicken pieces are patted dry with kitchen paper before you fry them or the oil will spit.

Fat Type
The chicken contains saturated fats in small amounts, the remainder is polyunsaturated fat.

SERVES 4

TROUT IN APSIC

This attractive main course is ideal for serving as a part of a summer's meal.

1.8 lts/3 pints water
Pinch salt
6 black peppercorns
2 bay leaves
2 sprigs fresh parsley
1 small onion, quartered
280ml/½ pint dry white wine
4 even-sized rainbow trout, gutted and well washed
2 egg whites, softly beaten
30g/2 tbsps powdered gelatin
Lemon slices, capers and sprigs of fresh dill, to garnish

1. Put the water, salt, peppercorns, bay leaves, parsley, onion and wine into a large saucepan or fish kettle. Bring to the boil and simmer for about 30 minutes.

2. Cool slightly, then lay the fish into the hot stock. Cover the pan and bring back to simmering point.

3. Cook the fish gently for 5 minutes, then remove from the heat.

4. Allow the fish to cool in the covered pan before removing and draining on absorbent kitchen paper.

5. Reserve the stock.

6. Using a sharp knife, carefully peel away the skin from the cooked fish.

7. Using a palette knife, lift the fillets from the top of each fish, taking great care that they do not break, and lay them on a large serving dish that has a slight well in the centre.

8. Lift the backbone away from the lower fillets and discard.

9. Arrange the lower fish fillets on the serving dish along with the others.

10. Strain the reserved fish stock into a large saucepan through a nylon sieve to remove the spices, herbs and vegetables.

11. Add the egg whites to the fish stock and heat gently, whisking constantly with a balloon whisk.

12. While you are whisking, the egg whites should form a thick frosty crust on top which removes all particles from the stock.

13. Bring the mixture to the boil then stop whisking and allow the egg whites and liquid to rise up the sides of the pan. Remove from the heat and allow to subside. Repeat this process twice more, then allow to settle completely.

14. Line a colander with several thicknesses of kitchen paper or muslin and stand the colander over a large bowl. Pour the fish stock into the colander along with the egg whites and allow to drain slowly. Do not allow the egg whites to fall into the clarified liquid.

15. When the liquid has drained through, remove about 280ml/¼ pint and heat it gently. Sprinkle over the gelatin and allow to stand until the gelatin has dissolved completely.

16. Mix the gelatin mixture into the remaining stock and allow to cool in a refrigerator until just beginning to set.

17. Decorate the trout and the base of the dish with the lemon slices, capers and dill.

18. When the aspic has become syrupy and slightly thickened, spoon it carefully over the fish fillets for decoration.

19. Place the serving plate into a refrigerator and chill until set (about 1-2 hours).

Cook's Notes

Time
Preparation takes 45 minutes to 1 hour. Total cooking time is about 50 minutes plus at least 1 hour to chill the dish.

Watchpoint
Do not stir or whisk the aspic or bubbles will form and these will set in the jelly and spoil the appearance. For speed you can use powdered aspic, available from most delicatessens.

Fat Type
Fish contains mono-unsaturated fats, and there are no other fats in this recipe.

SERVES 6

TURKEY KEBABS

For this low fat dish, use the ready-prepared turkey joints which are now easily available from supermarkets or butchers.

1.25kg/3lbs lean turkey meat
10ml/2 tsps fresh chopped sage
1 sprig rosemary, chopped
Juice 1 lemon
30ml/2 tbsps olive oil
Salt and freshly ground black pepper
120g/4oz lean back bacon, rind removed
Whole sage leaves

1. Remove any bone from the turkey and cut the meat into even-sized cubes.

2. Put the chopped sage, rosemary, lemon juice, oil, salt and pepper into a large bowl and stir in the turkey meat, mixing well to coat evenly. Cover and leave in the refrigerator overnight.

3. Cut the bacon strips into half lengthways and then again crosswise.

4. Wrap these pieces around as many of the cubes of marinated turkey meat as possible.

5. Thread the turkey and bacon rolls alternately with the sage leaves and any unwrapped turkey cubes onto kebab skewers.

6. Heat the grill to moderate, and cook the kebabs under the heat for 30 minutes, turning frequently and basting with the marinade whilst cooking. Serve immediately.

Step 3 Cut the bacon slices in half lengthways and then again crosswise.

Step 2 Stir the cubed turkey pieces into the marinade, mixing well to coat evenly.

Step 4 Carefully roll each piece of marinated turkey in a strip of bacon.

Cook's Notes

Time
Preparation takes 20 minutes, plus overnight soaking.
Cooking takes about 30 minutes.

Variation
Use chicken if preferred.

Serving Idea
Serve with pitta bread and salad, or on a bed of rice.

Fat Type
Both chicken and turkey contain low amounts of saturated fat. The bacon contains saturated fat, but this will be reduced whilst grilling.

SERVES 6

GREEN GRAPE SHORTCAKE

Plenty of fibre in the diet will help to reduce the amount of cholesterol found in the blood, and the wholemeal flour and grape skins in this recipe are a good source of fibre.

60g/2oz polyunsaturated margarine
30g/1oz soft brown sugar
60g/2oz wholemeal flour
30 g/1 oz ground almonds
225g/8oz green grapes, halved and pitted
570ml/1 pint water
Thinly pared rind of 2 lemons
15ml/1 tbsp honey
15g/½oz powdered gelatin
Few drops yellow food colouring, optional

1. Put the margarine, sugar, flour and almonds into a large bowl.

2. Work the margarine into the dry ingredients using your fingertips, and pressing the mixture together gently to form a soft dough.

3. Knead the dough lightly until it is smooth.

4. Line the base of a 20cm/8-inch loose-bottomed cake tin with silicone paper. Press the shortcake dough evenly over the base of the lined tin, making sure that it is pushed well into the sides.

5. Bake in a preheated oven 190°C/375°F/Gas Mark 5 for 15 minutes, or until the shortcake is firm and golden brown. Remove from the oven and allow to cool in the tin.

6. Lightly oil the inside of the cake tin above the shortcake with a little vegetable oil.

7. Arrange the grape halves on top of the shortcake.

8. Put the pint of water and lemon rind into a small pan and bring to the boil. Allow to simmer for 5 minutes, then remove the pan from the heat and allow the liquid to cool completely.

9. Strain the lemon liquid through a nylon sieve to remove the rinds. Measure off 450ml/¾ pint of the strained liquid and stir in the honey.

10. Put the remaining lemon liquid into a small saucepan and heat gently until it is very hot, but not boiling.

11. Sprinkle over the gelatin and allow to stand until it has completely dissolved.

Step 7 Arrange the grape halves over the cooked shortcake whilst it is still in the tin.

12. At this stage the food colouring can be added to the liquid if desired.

13. Stir the gelatin mixture into the lemon and honey mixture and stand in a cool place until it is beginning to set.

14. Spoon the partially set jelly carefully over the grapes making sure that they remain evenly spread.

15. Stand the shortcake in a refrigerator until the jelly has set completely. Serve in wedges.

Cook's Notes

Time
Preparation takes 45 minutes, plus cooling and chilling. Cooking takes about 20 minutes.

Preparation
It is important never to boil gelatin or it will not dissolve completely.

Fat Type
The fat in this recipe is polyunsaturated.

SERVES 6

PLUM AND HONEY COBBLER

A cobbler is a traditional dessert, so called because of the scones which decorate the top are reminiscent of the cobbles found on old roads.

1kg/2lbs ripe plums, halved and stoned
60-120ml/4-6 tbsps clear honey
225g/8oz wholemeal self-raising flour
30ml/2 tbsps caster sugar
60g/2oz polyunsaturated margarine
75-120ml/5-6 tbsps skimmed milk
1 egg, beaten

1. Put the plums into an ovenproof dish along with the honey. Cover with a sheet of foil and cook in a preheated oven 200°C/400°F/Gas Mark 6 for 20 minutes.

2. After this time the plums should be soft and a certain amount of juice should have formed in the dish. Remove from the oven and cool completely.

3. Put the flour and the sugar into a large bowl and using your fingers, rub in the margarine until the mixture resembles fine breadcrumbs.

4. Using a round bladed knife, stir in the milk and eggs, so that the mixture forms a soft dough.

5. Turn the dough out onto a lightly floured work surface and knead it until it is smooth.

6. Roll the dough out until it is about 1.5cm/½-inch thick.

7. Cut the dough into rounds using a 5cm/2-inch cutter to form the cobbles.

8. Carefully arrange the scone cobbles in a circle around

Step 4 Mix the milk and egg into the flour using a round bladed knife, and pressing all ingredients together to form a soft dough.

Step 8 Arrange a circle of scone cobbles around the top edge of the dish, overlapping each one slightly.

the top edge of the dish of plums, overlapping each scone slightly.

9. Brush the top of each scone with a little milk and sprinkle with a little extra sugar. Return the plum cobbler to the oven, set at the same temperature as before, and cook until the scones are firm, risen and well browned.

10. Serve hot.

Cook's Notes

Time
Preparation takes 30 minutes, cooking takes 45 minutes.

Variation
Use any variation of fresh fruit in place of the plums.

Serving Idea
This dessert is delicious hot with a scoop of vanilla ice cream, but do check the fat content of the ice cream first.

Fat Type
The fats used in recipe are polyunsaturated.

SERVES 6

CARIBBEAN FRUIT SALAD

This fruit salad is made from a refreshing mixture of tropical fruits, all of which are now easily available in most supermarkets.

½ cantaloup or honeydew melon, seeds removed
½ small pineapple
120g/4oz fresh strawberries
1 mango
225g/8oz water melon
120g/4oz guava
2 oranges
120g/4oz caster sugar
140ml/¼ pint white wine
Grated rind and juice of 1 lemon

1. Using a melon baller or teaspoon, scoop out rounds of flesh from the cantaloup or honeydew melon.

2. Cut the piece of pineapple in half lengthways and carefully peel away the outer skin.

3. Remove any eyes left in the outside edge of the pineapple using a potato peeler.

4. Cut away the core from the pineapple with a serrated knife and slice the flesh thinly. Put the slices of pineapple into a large bowl along with the melon rounds.

5. Hull the strawberries and halve them. Add them to the bowl with the pineapple and melon.

6. Peel the mango, and carefully cut the flesh away from the long stone in the centre of the fruit. Slice the flesh lengthways, and stir it into the bowl of fruit.

7. Peel the watermelon and guavas, then cube the flesh. Stir these into the bowl of fruit.

8. Remove the rind from the oranges using a serrated knife. Take care to remove all the white pith, or this will flavour the fruit salad.

9. Cut the orange into segments, carefully removing the inner membrane from the segments as you slice.

10. Put the sugar, wine, lemon juice and rind into a small saucepan and warm through gently, stirring all the time until the sugar has dissolved. Do not boil, then set aside to cool.

11. Put the syrup into the bowl along with the fruit and mix thoroughly. Chill the fruit salad completely before serving.

Step 3 Remove any eyes which remain in the pineapple flesh with the pointed end of a potato peeler.

Step 6 Carefully cut the flesh away from the long inner stone of the mango, before slicing it lengthways.

Cook's Notes

Time
Preparation takes 45 minutes, cooking takes about 3 minutes.

Fat Type
There are no fats at all in this recipe.

Preparation
It is unnecessary to remove the pips from the watermelon unless you particularly dislike them.

Watchpoint
Do not boil the syrup otherwise the flavour of the wine will be reduced.

LOW
SALT

Introduction

The mineral sodium chloride, or salt, has been used over the centuries for its medicinal properties as well as its flavouring and preserving qualities. Why then should we want a low salt diet? To answer this we must look more closely at the need for and the use of salt by our bodies.

Salt is essential to the balance of acids in the blood and the maintenance of the fluid content of our cells. Without a certain amount of salt we would suffer from severe muscular cramps and bodily degeneration. The quantity that our bodies require, however, is actually very small and is easily obtainable from the whole, fresh foods we eat daily without the need to add more.

The correct balance of salt in the body is maintained by the kidneys, which remove excess salt. Too great a salt intake can lead to fluid retention, places a strain on the kidneys and can even lead to problems such as depression.

More commonly, though, high sodium levels in the body can be directly linked to abnormally high blood pressure, or hypertension. All Western countries with a high salt consumption have a problem with high blood pressure. This, along with obesity and smoking, has been found to be one of the major causes of fatal heart disease.

Unfortunately, the taste for salt is addictive and people tend to feel that their bodies require large amounts. Whilst this may be true in a few instances, under normal conditions this is simply not the case. People simply become accustomed to the excessive use of salt and feel that without it their food lacks taste. Gradually their bodies remove less of the excess sodium and problems begin.

In this book, the recipes rely on alternative flavourings to enhance the taste of food. These ingredients may not have been available in ancient times when the taste for salt was established, but they are now easy to obtain. The recipes are simple to prepare and show just how easily you can adapt to a pattern of eating that will, with time, reduce your need for the flavour of salt.

MAKES 24

Cheesy Avocado Savouries

A delightful combination of avocado, nuts and cheese, this recipe doesn't need the addition of salt to enhance the taste of these delicious party savouries.

1 ripe avocado
30ml/2 tbsps single cream or natural yogurt
1 clove garlic, crushed
5ml/1 tsp lemon juice
90g/3oz finely grated Cheddar cheese
5ml/1 tsp ready-made English mustard
30g/1oz fresh white breadcrumbs
3 spring onions, finely chopped
Freshly ground black pepper, to taste
30ml/2 tbsps freshly chopped parsley
60g/2oz toasted, chopped almonds

Step 5 Form teaspoonfuls of the avocado mixture into small balls using your hands.

Step 7 Roll each ball into the finely chopped parsley, coating them thoroughly.

Step 1 After cutting, carefully twist the avocado apart to make two halves.

1. Cut the avocado in half lengthways and carefully twist it apart.

2. Remove the stone afd peel away the skin from the avocado halves using a sharp knife.

3. Mash the avocado flesh into a medium-sized bowl using a fork or a small potato masher.

4. Stir the cream or yogurt, garlic, lemon juice, grated cheese, mustard, breadcrumbs, onions and pepper into the mashed avocado. Mix together well with a fork until a stiff paste results.

5. Using your hands, roll teaspoonfuls of the avocado mixture into small balls.

6. Spread the parsley onto one small plate and the almonds onto another.

7. Roll half the number of avocado balls into the finely chopped parsley pressing it gently into the surface to coat thoroughly.

8. Roll the remaining avocado balls into the almonds in the same manner.

9. Refrigerate the coated snacks for 40 minutes before serving with drinks.

Cook's Notes

 Time
Preparation takes 30 minutes, plus 30 minutes refrigeration time.

 Preparation
It is most important to keep the mixture cool when preparing these snacks. If you have difficulty forming the mixture into small balls, refrigerate for at least 30 minutes.

 Variation
Use finely chopped walnuts instead of the almonds, and Stilton cheese instead of the Cheddar.

MAKES 36

STUFFED EGGS

Stuffed eggs make an attractive, and deliciously different, party appetiser.

18 small eggs, or quail eggs
60g/2oz unsalted butter
1 clove garlic, crushed
90g/3oz cooked, peeled prawns, finely chopped
2.5ml/½ tsp finely chopped fresh basil
Freshly ground black pepper, to taste

1. Cook the eggs in boiling water for 5 minutes. Drain, and plunge them immediately into cold water.

2. Allow the eggs to cool completely, then remove the shells. Rinse and drain.

3. Cut each egg in half lengthways and carefully remove the yolks.

4. Put the yolks into a large bowl and beat in the butter and garlic. Mix well.

5. Add the prawns, basil and pepper to the creamed egg yolk mixture. Beat thoroughly until a soft consistency results.

6. Fill each egg white half with a little of the prepared mixture, piling it attractively into the cavity left by the egg yolk.

7. Refrigerate until required.

Step 4 Cream the butter and garlic into the egg yolks, beating thoroughly to mix well.

Step 3 Using a sharp knife, halve the hard-boiled eggs lengthways.

Step 6 Pile equal amounts of the filling mixture into the halved egg whites, forking it attractively to serve.

Cook's Notes

Time
Preparation takes 15 minutes, cooking takes 5 minutes.

Variation
Use flaked white crab meat instead of the prawns. For a more exotic dish, use quails eggs instead of hens' eggs.

Serving Idea
Serve the filled egg halves on a plate which has been garnished with frisee lettuce leaves, and tiny pieces of red pepper.

MAKES 350g/12oz

SPICED NUTS

Everyone likes to nibble nuts with drinks at a party, but most contain very high quantities of salt. These delicious spiced nuts contain no salt, are extremely easy to make, and can be prepared well in advance.

30ml/2 tbsps corn or vegetable oil
120g/4oz fresh peanuts, shelled and husked
120g/4oz blanched almonds
120g/4oz fresh cashew nuts, shelled and husked
2.5ml/½ tsp ground ginger
2.5ml/½ tsp ground cinnamon
2.5ml/½ tsp cayenne pepper

1. Heat the oil in a large frying pan.

Step 3 Sprinkle the spices over the nuts and mix well.

Step 2 Stir the nuts into the hot oil, making sure they are evenly coated.

Step 4 Spread the nuts in an even layer on an ovenproof baking dish.

2. Stir in the nuts, mixing well to coat evenly with the hot oil.

3. Sprinkle the spices over the nuts and stir well to coat evenly.

4. Transfer the nuts to an ovenproof dish, spreading them in an even layer.

5. Toast the nuts for 10-15 minutes in a preheated oven, 190°C/375°F/Gas Mark 5.

6. To prevent the nuts from burning, turn them with a fish slice or palette knife once or twice during the cooking time.

Cook's Notes

Time
Preparation takes 10 minutes, cooking takes 10-15 minutes.

Cook's Tip
Prepare these nuts in advance and store them for up to 2 weeks in an airtight container.

Variation
Use hazelnuts instead of cashew nuts, and ground cardamom, cumin and chilli powder instead of the ginger, cinnamon and cayenne pepper.

SERVES 4-6
SPICY CHILLI BEAN SOUP

This 'complete meal' soup certainly doesn't need salt to bring out the full flavour of the ingredients.

90ml/3 tbsps vegetable oil
2 onions, roughly chopped
1 clove garlic, crushed
15ml/1 tbsp ground cumin
10ml/2 tsps ground paprika
1 red or green chilli pepper, seeded and finely chopped
225g/8oz minced beef
790g/1¾lbs canned tomatoes, chopped
860ml/1½ pints chicken or vegetable stock
90g/3oz tomato purée
5ml/1 tsp oregano
1 bay leaf
140ml/¼ pint beer
Freshly ground black pepper
120g/4oz each of canned red kidney beans, chick peas, and white pinto beans, drained and thoroughly rinsed.

1. Heat the oil in a large, heavy-based saucepan.

2. Add the onion and garlic and cook slowly until they become transparent.

3. Stir in the cumin, paprika and chilli pepper. Increase the heat and cook quickly for 30 seconds, stirring all the time.

4. Add the meat and cook until lightly browned, breaking up any large pieces with a fork.

5. Add the tomatoes and their juice, the stock, tomato purée, oregano, bay leaf, beer and ground pepper. Stir well, then bring to the boil.

6. Cover and simmer for approximately 50 minutes, checking the level of liquid several times during the cooking and adding more water if the soup seems too dry.

7. During the last 15 minutes of cooking, add the drained beans, stirring them in to mix well.

Step 4 Add the meat and cook until lightly browned, breaking up any large pieces with a fork.

Step 7 Add the drained beans to the soup during the last 15 minutes of cooking time.

Cook's Notes

Time
Preparation takes 30 minutes, cooking takes 1 hour.

Freezing
This soup freezes well.

Cook's Tip
If you cannot buy canned beans and chick peas, use 60g/2oz each of dried beans. Soak them overnight and cook thoroughly for 1 hour before using in this recipe.

Serving Idea
Serve with a mixed garnish of chopped fresh tomatoes, chopped spring onions and cubed avocado which has been sprinkled with lemon juice.

SERVES 4-6

COURGETTE SOUP WITH LEMON

The fresh taste of lemon and courgettes makes a delicious soup which can be served either hot or cold.

1 medium-sized onion, thinly sliced
30ml/2 tbsps olive oil
450g/1lb courgettes, topped, tailed and sliced
Finely grated rind and juice of 1 large lemon
450ml/¾ pint chicken stock
Freshly ground black pepper
2 egg yolks
200ml/⅓ pint natural yogurt

1. In a large pan, fry the onion gently in the olive oil for 3 minutes until it is just transparent.

2. Add the courgettes and fry for a further 2-3 minutes.

Step 1 In a large pan gently fry the onion until it is just transparent.

3. Stir in all remaining ingredients except the egg yolks and yogurt, cover and simmer for 20 minutes.

4. Transfer the soup to a liquidiser or food processor, and blend until smooth.

Step 4 Blend the soup in a liquidiser, or food processor, until it is smooth.

Step 5 Mix together the egg yolks and yogurt in a small jug or bowl.

5. Mix the egg yolks into the yogurt and stir into the blended soup.

6. Reheat the soup gently, stirring all the time until it thickens.

7. Serve hot at this stage, or transfer to a refrigerator and chill thoroughly.

Cook's Notes

Time
Preparation takes 20 minutes, plus chilling time, cooking takes 25 minutes.

Serving Idea
Serve the soup with a garnish of thinly sliced courgettes and light French toasts.

Preparation
Great care must be taken not to boil the soup once the egg yolks have been added, otherwise the mixture will curdle.

Freezing
This soup can be frozen, but not after the egg yolks have been added. Freeze before this stage, defrost and then finish the recipe as described.

SERVES 4

SEVICHE

In this traditional Mexican dish the raw fish is 'cooked' in a mixture of oil and lime juice. Quick and easy to prepare, seviche makes a highly nutritious and very tasty appetizer.

450g/1lb fresh cod fillet
Juice and grated rind of 2 limes
1 small shallot, finely chopped
1 green chilli pepper, seeded and finely chopped
5ml/1 tsp ground coriander
1 small green pepper, seeded and sliced
1 small red pepper, seeded and sliced
15ml/1 tbsp freshly chopped parsley
15ml/1 tbsp freshly chopped coriander
4 spring onions, finely chopped
30ml/2 tbsps olive oil
Freshly ground black pepper
1 small lettuce, to serve

1. Carefully remove the skin from the cod fillets.

2. Using a sharp knife cut the fish into very thin strips across the grain.

3. Put the fish strips into a large bowl and pour over the lime juice.

4. Stir in the grated lime rind, shallot, chilli pepper and ground coriander. Mix well.

5. Cover the bowl with plastic wrap or a damp cloth and refrigerate for 24 hours, stirring occasionally during this

time to ensure that the fish remains well coated in the lime.

6. Mix the sliced peppers, spring onions and the fresh herbs together in a large bowl.

7. Put the fish mixture into a colander and drain off the juice.

8. Put the drained fish into the pepper mixture and stir in the oil, mixing well to coat evenly. Add freshly ground pepper to taste.

9. Finely shred the lettuce and arrange on a serving plate.

10. Spread the fish mixture attractively over the lettuce and serve immediately, garnished with slices of lime, if liked.

Step 2 Cut the cod fillet across the grain into very thin slices.

Step 5 After refrigerating for 24 hours, the fish should have a cooked appearance.

Step 1 Using a sharp knife, carefully remove the skin from the cod fillets.

Cook's Notes

Time
Preparation takes 20 minutes, plus 24 hours standing time.

Variation
Use hake or salmon in place of the cod in this recipe.

Serving Idea
As well as being an interesting appetizer, Seviche can also be served with pitta breads for a tasty lunch.

SERVES 6-8

TERRINE OF SPINACH AND CHICKEN

This superb terrine is ideal when you want to impress your guests with a delicious appetizer.

225g/8oz chicken breasts, boned and skinned
2 egg whites
120g/4oz fresh white breadcrumbs
450g/1lb fresh spinach, washed
15ml/1 tbsp each of fresh finely chopped chervil, chives and tarragon
Freshly ground black pepper
280ml/½ pint double cream
60g/2oz finely chopped walnuts
Pinch nutmeg

Step 4 The spinach should be cooked until it is just wilted, using only the water that clings to the leaves and adding no extra liquid.

1. Cut the chicken into small pieces.

2. Put the cut chicken, 1 egg white and half of the breadcrumbs into a food processor. Blend until well mixed.

3. Put the spinach into a large saucepan and cover with a tight-fitting lid.

4. Cook the spinach for 3 minutes, or until it has just wilted.

5. Remove the chicken mixture from the food processor and rinse the bowl.

6. Put the spinach into the food processor along with the herbs, the remaining egg white and breadcrumbs. Blend until smooth.

7. Season the chicken mixture with a little pepper and add half of the cream. Mix well to blend thoroughly.

8. Add the remaining cream to the spinach along with the walnuts and the nutmeg. Beat this mixture well to blend thoroughly.

9. Line a 450g/1lb loaf tin with greaseproof paper. Lightly oil this with a little vegetable oil.

10. Pour the chicken mixture into the base of the tin and spread evenly.

11. Carefully pour the spinach mixture over the chicken mixture, and smooth the top with a palette knife.

12. Cover the tin with lightly oiled aluminium foil and seal this tightly around the edges.

13. Stand the tin in a roasting dish and pour enough warm water into the dish to come halfway up the sides of the tin.

14. Cook the terrine in a preheated oven 160°C/325°F/ Gas Mark 3 for 1 hour, or until it is firm.

15. Put the terrine into the refrigerator and chill for at least 12 hours.

16. Carefully lift the terrine out of the tin and peel off the paper. To serve, cut the terrine into thin slices with a sharp knife.

Cook's Notes

Time
Preparation takes 25 minutes, cooking takes 1 hour.

Serving Idea
Serve slices of the terrine on individual serving plates garnished with a little salad.

Watchpoint
Do not overcook the terrine or attempt to cook it any more quickly than the recipe states, otherwise it will curdle and spoil.

SERVES 4

ANDALUCIAN AUBERGINES

This delicious aubergine dish is highly reminiscent of Andalucia in Spain where tomatoes, rice and tuna fish are very popular ingredients.

4 small aubergines
45ml/3 tbsps olive oil
1 small onion, finely chopped
1 clove garlic, crushed
120g/4oz cooked whole grain rice
200g/7oz can tuna in oil, drained and fish coarsely flaked
15ml/1 tbsp mayonnaise
5ml/1 tsp curry powder
4 fresh tomatoes, skinned, seeded and chopped
15ml/1 tbsp coarsely chopped parsley
Freshly ground black pepper

1. Cut the aubergines in half lengthways. Score the cut surfaces lightly with a sharp knife at regular intervals.

2. Brush the scored surface lightly with 1 tbsp of the olive oil and place the aubergines on a greased baking sheet.

3. Bake the aubergines in a preheated oven 190°C/375°F/Gas Mark 5, for 15 minutes, or until beginning to soften.

4. Cool the aubergines slightly, then carefully scoop the centre flesh from each half. Take care that you do not break the skin at this stage.

5. Fry the chopped onion gently in the remaining 30 ml/2 tbsps of olive oil for 3 minutes, or until they are just transparent.

6. Add the garlic and the aubergine flesh, and fry for a further 2 minutes. Season to taste with pepper.

Step 1 Taking care not to break the skins, score the cut surface of the aubergine halves at regular intervals with a sharp, pointed knife.

Step 4 Carefully scoop the baked aubergine flesh out of each half, keeping the skin shells intact.

7. Add the rice, flaked tuna, mayonnaise, curry powder, tomatoes, parsley and black pepper to the aubergine mixture, and mix together well.

8. Pile equal amounts of this rice and tuna filling into the aubergine shells. Return the filled aubergines to the ovenproof baking dish. Brush with the remaining olive oil, and bake in the oven for a further 25 minutes. Serve piping hot.

Cook's Notes

Time
Preparation will take 40 minutes, cooking takes about 50 minutes.

Serving Idea
Serve with a crisp mixed leaf salad and black olives.

Preparation
Use a serrated grapefruit knife to remove the baked aubergine flesh without tearing the skins.

Variation
For a tasty vegetarian variation, use 175g/6oz button mushrooms in place of the tuna.

MAKES 1

HAM AND GREEN PEPPER OMELETTE

Use 'tendersweet' ham in this recipe to keep the salt content as low as possible.

3 eggs
30ml/2 tbsps milk
Freshly ground black pepper
15ml/1 tbsp vegetable oil
30g/1oz chopped green pepper
2 tomatoes, peeled, seeded and roughly chopped
60g/2oz lean ham, cut into small dice

1. Break the eggs into the bowl and beat in the milk and pepper.

2. Heat the oil in a omelette pan and fry the green pepper until it is just soft.

3. Stir in the tomatoes and the ham. Heat through for 1 minute.

4. Pour the egg mixture into the frying pan over the vegetables. Stir the mixture briskly with a wooden spoon, until it begins to cook.

5. As the egg begins to set, lift it slightly and tilt the pan to allow the uncooked egg underneath.

6. When the egg on top is still slightly creamy, fold the omelette in half and slip it onto a serving plate. Serve immediately

Step 5 Lift the cooked egg with a fork and tilt the frying pan to allow uncooked egg underneath.

Step 2 Gently fry the pepper in hot oil until it begins to soften.

Step 6 Fold the omelette in half whilst the top of the egg is still slightly creamy.

Cook's Notes

Time
Preparation takes about 15 minutes, cooking takes 5 minutes.

Serving Idea
Serve the omelette with a crisp leaf salad and French bread.

Cook's Tip
To peel tomatoes easily, cut a small cross into the skin and drop them into boiling water for about 10 seconds, then plunge into cold water. This loosens the peel.

Variation
Use any selection of your favourite vegetables to vary this delicious dish.

SERVES 4

TOMATOES PROVENÇALE

Use fragrant herbs from the Provence region of France to complement sweet tomatoes, and no salt will be required to enhance their flavour.

4 large ripe tomatoes
30ml/2 tbsps olive oil
1 clove garlic, crushed
2x1.25cm/½-inch-thick slices white bread, crusts removed
15ml/1 tbsp chopped parsley
10ml/2 tsps chopped thyme or marjoram
Freshly ground black pepper

Step 1 Using a grapefruit knife, carefully scoop the flesh out of each tomato half, making sure that you do not break the shells.

1. Cut the tomatoes in half and carefully cut out the tomato pulp using a grapefruit knife.

2. Put the tomato pulp into a sieve and press out the juice using the back of a wooden spoon. Put the dry tomato pulp into a large bowl.

3. Mix the olive oil and garlic together. Brush both sides of the bread with this mixture and leave to stand for 10 minutes.

4. Using a sharp knife, chop the oiled bread and the herbs together until they are well mixed and fine textured.

Stir this into the tomato pulp and add black pepper.

5. Press the tomato filling into the tomato shells, piling it slightly above the cut edge.

Step 2 Put the tomato pulp into a sieve and press out as much juice as possible using the back of a wooden spoon.

Step 4 Using a sharp knife, chop the herbs and the oiled bread together until they are as fine as breadcrumbs.

6. Arrange the tomatoes on an ovenproof dish and grill under a low heat for 5 minutes.

7. Raise the temperature of the grill to high and brown the tomatoes on top for a few seconds. Serve at once.

Cook's Notes

Time
Preparation takes 15-20 minutes. Cooking time takes 5 minutes.

Cook's Tip
Prepare the tomatoes in advance and grill them just before serving.

Serving Idea
Serve with a rice salad for a light lunch.

SERVES 4-6
MUSHROOM SALAD

Mushrooms have a flavour all of their own and do not require salt.
This salad can be made using cultivated
mushrooms, but it is extra special when prepared with wild ones.

450g/1lb button or oyster mushrooms
1 medium-sized onion
45ml/3 tbsps vegetable oil
15ml/1 tbsp freshly chopped parsley
1 cucumber, finely diced
3-4 tomatoes, peeled, seeded and sliced
60ml/4 tbsps olive oil
15ml/1 tbsp white wine vinegar
Freshly ground black pepper
1 small iceberg lettuce

1. Trim the mushrooms and rub clean with a damp cloth.

2. Slice the mushrooms very thinly and chop the onions finely.

Step 2 Slice the mushrooms very thinly with a sharp knife.

3. Heat the vegetable oil in a large frying pan and gently sauté the mushrooms and onions for 2-3 minutes, or until they are just soft. Allow to cool.

Step 3 Fry the mushrooms and onions gently in hot oil until they just begin to soften.

Step 4 Add the parsley, cucumber and tomatoes to the mushrooms, mixing well to combine ingredients evenly.

4. When the mushrooms have cooled, stir in the parsley, cucumber and tomatoes.

5. Mix together the oil, vinegar and pepper in a small jug, and pour over all the other ingredients.

6. Stir gently to coat evenly, and refrigerate for 1-2 hours.

7. Shred the lettuce finely and arrange on a serving plate. Spread the chilled mushrooms evenly over the lettuce.

Cook's Notes

Time
Preparation takes 10 minutes, cooking takes 5 minutes. Chilling time is a minimum of 2 hours.

Cook's Tip
The salad can be prepared a day in advance and stored in the refrigerator until required.

Serving Ideas
Serve with Melba toast or crusty wholemeal rolls.

SERVES 4

SZECHWAN MEATBALLS

*Szechwan is a region of China that lends its name to a style of
cookery which includes many spices, most notably ginger.
The spicy nature of these dishes means they require no salt.*

90g/3oz blanched almonds
450g/1lb minced beef
5ml/1 tsp grated fresh ginger
1 clove garlic, crushed
½ large green pepper, seeded and chopped
Dash of Szechwan, chilli, or Tabasco sauce
30ml/2 tbsps soy sauce
Oil for frying
45ml/3 tbsps soy sauce
120ml/4 fl oz vegetable stock
15ml/1 tbsp rice wine or white wine vinegar
10ml/2 tsps honey
15ml/1 tbsp sherry
15ml/1 tbsp cornflour
4 spring onions, sliced diagonally

blended.

4. Divide the mixture into16 and roll each piece into small meatballs on a lightly floured board.

5. Heat a little oil in a large frying pan and lay in about half of the meatballs in a single layer.

6. Cook the meatballs over a low heat for about 20 minutes, turning them frequently until they are well browned all over.

7. Transfer to a serving dish and keep warm while you cook the remaining meatballs. Set aside as before.

8. Stir the 3 tbsps soy sauce, stock and vinegar into the frying pan and bring to the boil. Boil briskly for about 30 seconds.

Step 1 Toast the almonds under a low grill until pale gold in colour, stirring them frequently to prevent them from burning.

Step 6 Gently fry the meatballs in the hot oil until they are evenly browned.

1. Spread the almonds evenly onto a grill pan, and grill under a low heat for 3-4 minutes, or until lightly toasted. Stir the almonds often to prevent them from burning.

2. Chop the almonds coarsely using a large sharp knife.

3. In a large bowl, combine the chopped almonds with the meat, ginger, garlic, green pepper, Szechwan sauce, and the 2 tbsps of soy sauce. Use a wooden spoon, or your hands, to ensure that the ingredients are well

9. Add the honey and stir until dissolved.

10. Blend the sherry and cornflour together in a small bowl, and add this into the hot sauce. Cook, stirring all the time, until thickened.

11. Arrange the meatballs on a serving dish and sprinkle with the sliced spring onions. Pour the sauce over, and serve.

Cook's Notes

Time
Preparation takes about 20 minutes, cooking takes 40 minutes.

Serving Idea
Serve with boiled rice and a tomato salad.

Freezing
The meatballs will freeze uncooked for up to 3 months. The sauce should be prepared freshly when required.

SERVES 4-6

CHICKEN CACCIATORE

The use of herbs, wine and vinegar in this delicious Italian family meal gives a wonderful, hearty flavour without the need for salt.

60ml/4 tbsps olive oil
1.5kg/3lbs chicken pieces
2 onions, sliced
3 cloves garlic, crushed
225g/8oz button mushrooms, quartered
140ml/¼ pint red wine
15ml/1 tbsp wine vinegar
15ml/1 tbsp fresh chopped parsley
10ml/2 tsps fresh chopped oregano
10ml/2 tsps fresh chopped basil
1 bay leaf
450g/1lb tinned tomatoes
140ml/¼ pint chicken stock
Freshly ground black pepper
Pinch of sugar

1. In a large frying pan heat the oil and lay the chicken pieces, skin side down, in one layer.

2. Brown for 3-4 minutes, then turn each piece over.

Continue turning the chicken portions until all surfaces are well browned.

3. Remove the chicken portions to a plate and keep warm.

4. Add the onions and garlic to the oil and chicken juices in the frying pan. Cook lightly for 2-3 minutes, or until they are just beginning to brown.

5. Add the mushrooms to the pan and cook for about 1 minute, stirring constantly.

6. Pour the wine and vinegar into the pan and boil rapidly to reduce to about half the original quantity.

7. Add the herbs, bay leaf and tomatoes, stirring well to break up the tomatoes.

8. Stir in the chicken stock and season with pepper and sugar.

9. Return the chicken to the tomato sauce and cover with a tight fitting lid. Simmer for about 1 hour, or until the chicken is tender.

Step 2 Turn the chicken frequently until all the outer surfaces are golden brown.

Step 7 Break the tomatoes in the pan by pressing them gently with the back of a wooden spoon.

Cook's Notes

Time
Preparation takes about 20 minutes, cooking takes 1 hour 15 minutes.

Serving Idea
Serve with rice or pasta, and a mixed salad.

Variation
Use the delicious sauce in this recipe with any other meat of your choice.

Freezing
This dish freezes well for up to 3 months. Defrost thoroughly and reheat by simmering for at least 30 minutes before serving.

SERVES 4

SWEDISH HERRINGS

The Swedes adore the flavour of fresh dill and mild mustard.
This combination is all that is required
to bring out the full flavour of fresh herring.

60ml/4 tbsps fresh chopped dill
90ml/3 fl oz mild Swedish mustard
30ml/2 tbsps lemon juice or white wine
4-8 fresh herrings, cleaned, but heads and tails left on
30ml/2 tbsps unsalted butter, melted
Freshly ground black pepper
Lemon wedges and whole sprigs of fresh dill, to garnish

Step 2 Using a very sharp knife, cut 3 shallow slits just through the skin on each side of the fish.

Step 1 Mix the dill, mustard and lemon juice or white wine together in a small bowl, mixing well to blend all these ingredients thoroughly.

Step 3 Spread the mustard mixture over each fish, carefully pushing a little into each cut.

1. Put the dill, mustard and lemon juice or white wine into a small bowl and mix together thoroughly.

2. Using a sharp knife, cut three shallow slits through the skin on both sides of each fish.

3. Spread half of the mustard mixture over one side of each fish, pushing some of the mixture into each cut.

4. Drizzle a little of the melted butter over the fish and grill under a preheated hot grill for 5-6 minutes.

5. Using a fish slice, carefully turn each fish over, and spread with the remaining dill and mustard mixture.

6. Drizzle over the remaining butter and grill for a further 5-6 minutes, or until the fish is thoroughly cooked.

7. Sprinkle the fish with black pepper and serve garnished with the dill sprigs and lemon wedges.

Cook's Notes

Time
Preparation takes 10 minutes, cooking takes 12-15 minutes.

Cook's Tip
To be sure that the fish you are buying are completely fresh, make sure that the skins are moist and the eyes are bright.

Variation
Use mackerel instead of the herrings in this recipe.

Serving Idea
Serve with new potatoes and green vegetables.

SERVES 4

SWEET AND SOUR TURKEY MEATBALLS

These easy-to-prepare turkey meatballs are served with a highly flavoured sweet and sour sauce.

1 small onion, finely chopped
30ml/2 tbsps olive oil
450g/1lb raw turkey
1 clove garlic, peeled and crushed
30ml/2 tbsps fresh parsley, chopped
30ml/2 tbsps blanched almonds, finely chopped
Freshly ground black pepper
1.25ml/¼ tsp mixed spice
15ml/1 tbsp chopped raisins
30ml/2 tbsps fresh wholemeal breadcrumbs
1 egg, beaten
4 spring onions, thinly sliced
280ml/½ pint pure tomato juice
30ml/2 tbsps tomato purée
Juice of half a lemon
15ml/1 tbsp honey
1 green chilli, seeded and thinly sliced
2 slices fresh pineapple, finely chopped
1 medium-sized red pepper, seeded and cut into thin strips
2 carrots, peeled and coarsely grated

1. Fry the onions gently in the olive oil until they are just transparent.

2. Using a food processor or mincer, finely chop or mince the raw turkey.

3. Put the minced turkey into a large bowl, along with the garlic, parsley, almonds, pepper, mixed spice, raisins, breadcrumbs and egg.

4. Stir in the cooked onion and the oil, mixing well to combine all ingredients thoroughly.

5. Divide the mixture into 16 and shape each piece into a small ball. Chill for 30 minutes.

Step 4 Stir the fried onions and the oil into the minced turkey mixture, mixing thoroughly to ensure that all ingredients are blended evenly.

Step 5 Divide the mixture into 16 and shape each piece into a small ball using lightly floured hands.

6. Put all the remaining ingredients into a shallow pan and bring to the boil. Cover the pan and simmer the sauce gently for 10 minutes, stirring occasionally.

7. Carefully drop the chilled meatballs into the sauce. Re-cover and simmer for a further 20 minutes, or until the meatballs are completely cooked.

Cook's Notes

 Time
Preparation takes 20-25 minutes, cooking time takes about 35 minutes.

 Serving Idea
Serve with brown rice or wholemeal pasta.

 Preparation
If the sauce evaporates too quickly, add a little stock or water to keep it to a thin enough consistency.

 Cook's Tip
The shaped meatballs can be lightly fried in a little oil before being added to the sauce, if preferred.

SERVES 4

SKATE WINGS WITH BUTTER SAUCE

Fish of any kind is an excellent source of iodine for people who are on a low salt diet. Skate wings are both economical and delicious, and can make an interesting change from everyday fish dishes.

4 wings of skate
1 very small onion, sliced
2 parsley stalks
6 black peppercorns
280ml/½ pint vegetable or fish stock
60g/4 tbsps unsalted butter
15ml/1 tbsp capers
30ml/2 tbsps white wine vinegar
15ml/1 tbsp fresh chopped parsley

1. Place the skate wings in one layer in a large deep sauté pan.

2. Add the onion slices, parsley stalks and peppercorns, then pour over the stock.

3. Bring the fish gently to the boil with the pan uncovered and allow to simmer for 10-15 minutes.

4. Carefully remove the skate wings from the pan and arrange on a serving platter.

5. Remove any skin or large pieces of bone, taking great care not the break up the fish. Keep warm.

6. Place the butter into a small pan and cook over a high heat until it begins to brown.

7. Add the capers and immediately remove the butter from the heat. Stir in the vinegar to foam the hot butter.

8. Pour the hot butter sauce over the skate wings and sprinkle with some chopped parsley. Serve immediately.

Step 5 Carefully remove any skin or large bones from the cooked fish using a small sharp pointed knife.

Step 1 Place the skate wings in a pan along with the onion slice, parsley stalks, peppercorns and stock.

Step 7 Add the vinegar to the hot butter and capers. This will cause the butter to froth.

Cook's Notes

Time
Preparation takes 10-15 minutes, cooking will take 20 minutes.

Serving Idea
Serve with fresh vegetables and new or jacket potatoes.

Preparation
When the skate is completely cooked, the meat will pull away from the bones in long strips.

Watchpoint
Take care not to burn the butter when heating it rapidly. It should only just begin to brown, before adding the capers and vinegar.

SERVES 4

CHICKEN WITH APPLE CREAM SAUCE

Fresh tasting apples and tender chicken makes this low salt recipe ideal for serving as part of a special meal.

60g/2oz unsalted butter
30ml/2 tbsps vegetable oil
8 skinned and boned chicken breasts
60ml/4 tbsps brandy
2 dessert apples, peeled, cored and coarsely chopped
1 shallot, finely chopped
2 sticks celery, finely chopped
2.5ml/½ tsp dried thyme, crumbled
90ml/6 tbsps chicken stock
2 eggs, lightly beaten
90ml/6 tbsps double cream

---

1. Melt half the butter and all of the oil in a large sauté pan until it is foaming.

2. Add the chicken and fry gently, turning once or twice, until each piece is well browned.

3. Pour off most of the fat from the pan, leaving just the chicken pieces and their juices to cook.

4. Pour the brandy into the pan with the chicken and heat gently. Carefully ignite the brandy with a match and shake the sauté pan until the flames subside.

5. In a small saucepan or frying pan, melt the remaining butter. Stir in the chopped apple, shallot and celery. Cook for about 5 minutes, until soft, but not brown.

6. Add the cooked apples to the chicken portions, along with the thyme and stock. Bring the chicken to the boil, cover, reduce the heat and simmer for 30 minutes.

7. Remove the chicken from the pan and arrange on a serving dish. Put the eggs and cream into a bowl and gradually whisk in some of the hot sauce from the sauté pan. Continue whisking until all the hot sauce has been added and the mixture is smooth.

8. Return the sauce to the sauté pan and heat gently over a low temperature for 2-3 minutes, stirring constantly until the sauce thickens. Pour the hot sauce over the chicken breasts and serve garnished with some watercress.

Step 4 Carefully ignite the warmed brandy, shaking the pan gently until the flames subside.

Step 7 Whisking vigorously with a balloon whisk, gradually add the hot sauce mixture to the eggs and cream, beating until smooth.

Cook's Notes

Time
Preparation takes 25-30 minutes, cooking takes 40-50 minutes.

Preparation
If preferred, the sauce can be blended using a food processor or liquidiser instead of whisking by hand.

Serving Idea
Serve with sauté potatoes and petit pois.

Watchpoint
Take great care not to allow the sauce to boil once the egg and cream is added or it will curdle.

SERVES 4

MEDITERRANEAN SHELLFISH CASSEROLE

Fresh shellfish cooked with red wine and tomatoes makes an impressive main course to serve for that special dinner party.

1 onion, peeled and finely chopped
2 cloves garlic, peeled and crushed
45ml/3 tbsps olive oil
750g/1½lbs tomatoes, skinned, seeded and chopped
30ml/2 tbsps tomato purée
570ml/1 pint dry red wine
Freshly ground black pepper
1¼ ltrs/2 pints mussels, in their shells
8 large Mediterranean prawns, in their shells
120g/4oz peeled prawns
120g/4oz white crab meat
8 small crab claws, for garnish
30ml/2 tbsps vegetable oil
1 clove garlic, crushed
1 tbsp fresh chopped parsley
8 slices stale French bread

1. In a large saucepan, fry the onion gently in the olive oil for 3 minutes, or until transparent but not browned.

2. Add the 2 cloves of garlic and chopped tomatoes to the onions, fry gently for a further 3 minutes, stirring to break up the tomatoes.

3. Stir in the tomato purée, red wine and black pepper. Bring the sauce to the boil; cover and simmer for 15 minutes.

4. Scrub the mussels to remove any small barnacles or bits of seaweed attached to the shells.

5. If any of the mussels are open, tap them gently with the handle of a knife. If they do not close up immediately, discard.

6. Drop all tightly closed mussels into the simmering tomato sauce. Cover and cook for 5 minutes.

Step 4 Trim any small barnacles or pieces of seaweed away from the mussel shells using a small, sharp knife.

Step 6 After cooking for 5 minutes in the tomato sauce, all the mussels should have opened completely. Any that do not, must be removed and discarded.

7. Add the whole prawns, peeled prawns, crab and claws to the mussels and tomatoes. Re-cover and simmer for 5 minutes.

8. Heat the vegetable oil in a frying pan and stir in the remaining garlic clove and parsley.

9. Put the slices of French bread into the hot oil and fry until brown on one side. Turn each slice over and fry until the second side is well browned.

10. Spoon the fish stew into a deep sided serving dish and arrange the garlic croutons over the top. Stir briefly before serving.

Cook's Notes

Time
Preparation takes 15-20 minutes, cooking takes about 30 minutes.

Preparation
All the mussels must have opened completely after being cooked in the tomato sauce. Any that do not, must be removed and discarded.

Serving Idea
Serve with a large mixed salad and perhaps some extra French bread to mop up the sauce.

SERVES 6

VEAL WITH SORREL AND CHEESE STUFFING

*Fresh sorrel has a delightful flavour and is often found growing
wild in the countryside or in old back gardens.
If you cannot get any, use fresh spinach instead.*

900g/2lbs rolled joint of veal
120g/4oz Philadelphia cheese with garlic and herbs
120g/4oz sorrel leaf, finely chopped
10ml/2 tsps fresh oregano or marjoram, chopped
60g/2oz finely chopped walnuts
Freshly ground black pepper
60g/2oz plain flour
2.5ml/½ tsp paprika
1 egg, beaten
120g/4oz dried breadcrumbs
45ml/3 tbsps unsalted butter, melted

Step 2 Spread the filling ingredients evenly over the inside of the joint of meat.

1. Unroll the veal joint and trim off some of the fat from the outside using a sharp knife.

2. Put the cheese, sorrel, oregano or marjoram, walnuts and black pepper into a bowl. Mix together using a round bladed knife or your hands, until the ingredients are well bound together. Spread this filling over the inside of the veal.

3. Roll the veal joint up, swiss-roll fashion, and sew the ends together with a trussing needle and thick thread.

4. Dredge the veal roll with the flour and sprinkle with the paprika. Press this coating well onto the meat using your hands.

5. Brush the floured joint liberally with beaten egg and roll it into the dried breadcrumbs, pressing gently to make sure that all surfaces are thoroughly coated.

Step 3 Sew the ends of the joint together using a trussing needle and strong thread.

6. Place the coated veal on a baking sheet, brush with melted butter and roast in a preheated oven 160°C/325°F/Gas Mark 5, for 1 hour, or until the meat is well cooked.

7. Allow to stand for 10 minutes before slicing and serving hot, or chill and serve cold.

Cook's Notes

 Time
Preparation takes 25 minutes, cooking takes 1-1½ hours.

 Variation
Use a rolled joint of lamb instead of the veal.

 Serving Idea
Serve with salad or vegetables and a rich brown sauce.

 Freezing
This recipe will freeze well, and is ideal prepared in advance and served cold, after being thawed.

SERVES 4

POUSSINS WITH DEVILLED SAUCE

Although this recipe takes quite a while to prepare, the end result will make your effort worthwhile.

4 poussins
5ml/1 tsp each of paprika, mustard powder and ground ginger
2.5ml/½ tsp ground turmeric
1.25ml/¼ tsp ground allspice
60g/4 tbsps unsalted butter
30ml/2 tbsps chilli sauce
15ml/1 tbsp plum chutney
15ml/1 tbsp brown sauce
15ml/1 tbsp Worcestershire sauce
15ml/1 tbsp soy sauce
Dash Tabasco sauce
45ml/3 tbsps chicken stock

1. Tie the legs of each poussin together and tuck them under the wing tips.

2. Put the paprika, mustard, ginger, turmeric and allspice, into a small bowl and mix together well.

3. Rub the spice mixture evenly on all sides of the four poussins, taking great care to push some behind the wings and into the joints.

4. Refrigerate the poussins for at least 1 hour.

5. Arrange the poussins in a roasting pan. Melt the butter and brush it evenly over the birds. Roast in a preheated oven, 180°C/350°F/Gas Mark 4, for 20 minutes, brushing with the roasting juices during this time.

6. Put the chilli sauce, plum chutney, brown sauce, Worcestershire sauce, soy sauce and Tabasco and chicken stock into a small bowl and mix well.

7. Brush about half of this sauce over the poussins. Return to the oven and cook for a further 40 minutes.

8. Brush the poussins twice more with the remaining sauce mixture during this final cooking time so that the skins become brown and crisp.

Step 1 Tie the legs of each poussin together with trussing thread and tuck them under the wing tips.

Step 3 Rub the poussins all over with the spice mixture, pressing it down into the wings and joints.

Cook's Notes

 Time
Preparation takes about 25 minutes, plus 1 hour standing time. Cooking takes 60-70 minutes, depending on the size of the poussins.

 Variation
Use pigeons or grouse instead of the poussins in this recipe.

 Serving Idea
Serve with fresh cooked pasta and a large salad.

 Freezing
This dish freezes well for up to 3 months.

SERVES 4

FIVE-SPICED PORK

Five spice is a ready-prepared spicy powder which can easily be obtained from delicatessens or ethnic supermarkets. It is used in this dish with ginger and pepper to make a typical Szechwan meal.

450g/1lb fillet pork
60ml/4 tbsps sesame oil
One 2.5cm/1-inch piece fresh ginger, peeled and chopped
5ml/1 tsp black peppercorns
5ml/1 tsp five spice powder
75ml/5 tbsps dry sherry
140ml/¼ pint light stock
30ml/2 tbsps honey
4 spring onions, cut into diagonal slices
60g/2oz bamboo shoots, shredded
1 large ripe mango, peeled and flesh sliced

1. Using a sharp knife, finely slice the pork fillets into thin strips.

Step 1 Using a sharp knife, shred the pork into thin strips.

2. Put the oil into a wok or large frying pan, and heat gently. Add the ginger and stir this into the oil. Fry quickly for 20-30 seconds.

Step 3 Stir-fry the meat with the oil and ginger.

Step 5 Add the onions, bamboo shoots and mango to the cooked pork, stirring continuously to cook evenly.

3. Add the sliced meat to the wok and stir-fry for 4-5 minutes, or until the meat is well cooked and tender.

4. Stir the peppercorns, five spice powder, sherry, stock and honey into the meat. Mix well and bring to the boil.

5. Add all the remaining ingredients to the wok and cook quickly, stirring all the time for a further 3 minutes.

6. Serve immediately.

Cook's Notes

Time
Preparation takes 25 minutes, cooking takes about 10 minutes.

Variation
Use chicken instead of pork in this recipe.

Serving Idea
Serve with rice or Chinese noodles.

SERVES 4

SWEET PEPPER STEAKS

*The sweet peppers in this recipe refer only to the vegetable and not
to the flavour of this dish. Peppers, mustard and capers blend
together to make a delicious spicy sauce without the need for added salt.*

4 sirloin steaks, approximately 120g/4oz each in weight
2 cloves garlic, crushed
Freshly ground black pepper
45ml/3 tbsps vegetable oil
2 shallots, finely chopped
60ml/4 tbsps capers
120g/4oz sliced mushrooms
30g/2 tbsps plain flour
280ml/½ pint dark stock
20ml/4 tsps ready-made mustard
10ml/2 tsps Worcestershire sauce
120ml/8 tbsps white wine
10ml/2 tsps lemon juice
Pinch each of dried thyme and rosemary
8 baby corn on the cobs, cut in half lengthways
1 green pepper, seeded and finely sliced
1 red pepper, seeded and finely sliced
1 yellow pepper, seeded and finely sliced
4 tomatoes, peeled, seeded and cut into thin strips

1. Lay the steaks onto a board and rub both surfaces of each with the garlic and black pepper. Refrigerate for 30 minutes.

2. Heat the oil in a large frying pan and quickly fry the steaks for 1 minute on each side. Remove the steaks from the pan and set aside.

3. Add the shallot, capers and mushrooms to the oil and meat juices in the frying pan. Cook for about 1 minute.

4. Sprinkle the flour over the vegetables and fry gently until it begins to brown. Pour over the stock and stir well, adding the mustard, Worcestershire sauce, wine, lemon juice, thyme and rosemary, as the sauce thickens.

5. Return the steaks to the sauce mixture along with the sweet corn, peppers and tomatoes. Simmer for 6-8 minutes, or until the steaks are cooked, but still pink in the centre. Serve at once.

Step 4 Sprinkle the flour over the cooked vegetables and fry gently to brown lightly.

Step 5 Stir the sweetcorn, peppers and tomatoes into the sauce, mixing well to coat evenly.

Cook's Notes

Time
Preparation takes about 30 minutes, plus 30 minutes chilling time. Cooking takes 20 minutes.

Preparation
It is important to fry the steaks initially on both sides as this helps to seal in the meats juices.

Serving Idea
Serve the steaks with rice or jacket potatoes.

SERVES 6

HONEY AND APPLE TART

This delicious apple flan is wonderful served either hot or cold.

90g/3oz wholemeal flour
90g/3oz plain white flour
90g/3oz unsalted butter
1 egg yolk
45ml/3 tbsps cold water
280ml/½ pint unsweetened apple purée
15ml/1 tbsp honey
2 egg yolks
30ml/2 tbsps ground almonds
3 large eating apples, quartered, cored and thinly sliced
Little pale soft brown sugar
45ml/3 tbsps clear honey, warmed to glaze

Step 4 Pinch the edges of the flan up, and prick the base with a fork.

1. Put the flours into a large bowl.

2. Cut the butter into small pieces and rub these into the flour until the mixture resembles fine breadcrumbs.

3. Beat the egg yolk and 30ml/2 tbsps of the water together. Stir this into the dry ingredients, mixing to a firm

soft dough and adding a little extra water if necessary.

4. Roll the dough on a lightly floured surface and line a 22.5 cm/9-inch loose-bottom, fluted flan ring. Pinch up the edges well and prick the base to prevent it from rising during cooking.

5. Mix the apple purée with the honey, egg yolks and ground almonds, stirring well to blend thoroughly.

6. Spread this apple mixture evenly over the base of the pastry case.

7. Arrange the apple slices, overlapping slightly, in circles on the top of the apple and almond filling.

Step 7 Arrange the apple slices, overlapping each slice slightly in circles, on the top of the apple and almond filling.

8. Sprinkle the top of the flan lightly with a little soft brown sugar, and bake in a preheated oven 190°C/375°F/Gas Mark 5 for 35-40 minutes, or until the apples are just beginning to go golden brown.

9. As soon as the flan is removed from the oven, carefully brush the top with the warmed honey glaze.

Cook's Notes

Time
Preparation takes 45 minutes, cooking takes about 40 minutes.

Serving Idea
Serve with fresh whipped cream.

Watchpoint
If the apples begin to brown before the end of cooking time, cover the tart with aluminium foil to prevent any further colouring.

SERVES 6-8

PRUNE, APRICOT AND NUT FLAN

This sumptuous sweet tart has a nutty shortcake pastry for its base.

120g/4oz dried apricots
120g/4oz dried prunes
280ml/½ pint red wine, or dry cider
120g/4oz unsalted butter
60g/2oz soft brown sugar
120g/4oz plain flour
60g/2oz ground hazelnuts
45ml/3 tbsps finely chopped walnuts
30ml/2 tbsps clear honey, warmed

Step 4 Work the chopped walnuts into the pastry as you knead it.

Step 3 Gradually fold the ground hazelnuts and flour into the creamed butter and sugar until it forms a soft dough.

Step 5 Press the shortcake pastry evenly over the base of a loose-bottomed flan tin.

1. Put the apricots and prunes into a large bowl. Warm the wine or cider, and pour it over the dried fruit. Leave to stand for 4 hours minimum.

2. Put the butter and sugar into a large bowl and cream it together until it becomes light and fluffy.

3. Gradually stir in the flour and ground hazelnuts.

4. Knead the dough lightly until it is smooth, working in the chopped walnuts as you go.

5. Press the shortcake dough evenly over the base of a 22.5cm/9-inch fluted loose-bottomed flan tin. Prick the surface of the dough with a fork and bake in a preheated oven, 190°C/375°F/Gas Mark 5, for 15 minutes.

6. Remove the prunes and apricots from the soaking liquid and drain them thoroughly on absorbent paper.

7. Remove the shortcake from the oven and arrange the fruit over the hot shortcake.

8. Cover the tart with aluminium foil and return to the oven for a further 10 minutes.

9. Remove the shortcake carefully from its tin and arrange on a serving plate.

10. While the shortcake is still hot, brush the fruit with the warmed honey to glaze.

Cook's Notes

Time
Preparation takes 30 minutes, plus soaking time. Cooking takes 25 minutes.

Watchpoint
If the shortcake mixture is too soft to handle, chill it in a refrigerator for 30 minutes.

Freezing
This dessert freezes well for up to 2 months, but should be glazed just before serving.

MAKES 10-12 TEACAKES

SAFFRON TEACAKES

The use of sweet spices in baking will reduce the necessity to add salt to recipes.

140ml/¼ pint milk
Good pinch saffron
225g/8oz self-raising flour
120g/4oz unsalted butter
120g/4oz currants
2.5ml/½ tsp allspice
30g/1oz candied peel
60g/2oz caster sugar
1 egg, beaten

1. Heat 60ml/4 tbsps of the milk in a small saucepan and add the saffron. Allow to stand for 10-15 minutes to infuse.

2. Sift the flour into a large bowl and cut the butter into this with a knife, until it is reduced to very small pieces.

3. Stir the currants, allspice, peel and sugar into the flour and butter mixture.

4. Make a well in the centre of the flour and stir in the saffron milk and the remainder of the milk. Mix well to form a soft dough

5. Turn the dough onto a lightly floured board, and knead until smooth.

6. Roll the dough into a circle approximately 1.25cm/½ -inch thick. Cut into 10-12 rounds with a 7.5cm/3-inch pastry cutter.

7. Arrange the individual rounds on a lightly greased baking sheet, and brush the top with a little beaten egg.

8. Bake the cakes in a preheated oven, 180°C/350°F/ Gas Mark 4, for 20-30 minutes, until they are well risen and golden brown.

Step 1 Allow the saffron to infuse in the hot milk until it is golden.

Step 2 Using a round-bladed knife, cut the butter into the flour until it is finely chopped.

Step 4 Mix the milk into the flour from the centre of the bowl, drawing the flour into the liquid gradually.

Cook's Notes

Time
Preparation takes 15 minutes, cooking will take 20-30 minutes.

Cook's Tip
Do not be tempted to use too much saffron; a little will go a very long way.

Freezing
These teacakes freeze very well for up to 1 month.

MAKES ONE 17.5cm/7-inch SQUARE CAKE

GINGERBREAD

Dark treacle and fresh ginger combine to make this favourite family cake.

120g/4oz unsalted butter
120ml/4 fl oz black treacle
225g/8oz light soft brown sugar
120ml/4 fl oz hot water
300g/10oz plain flour
10ml/2 tsps baking powder
10ml/2 tsps fresh ginger, peeled and grated
5ml/1 tsp grated nutmeg
1 egg, beaten

Step 4 Gradually beat in the treacle, using a wooden spoon and drawing the flour from the outside into the centre.

Step 1 Melt the butter, treacle and sugar together in a large saucepan.

Step 6 The cake is done when a skewer inserted into the centre comes out clean.

1. Put the butter into a large saucepan, along with the treacle and sugar. Heat gently, stirring all the time, until the sugar and butter have melted together.

2. Pour in the hot water, mix well and set aside.

3. Sift the flour with the baking powder into a large bowl. Make a well in the centre, and add the ginger, nutmeg and beaten egg.

4. Gradually beat in the treacle, using a wooden spoon and drawing the flour from the outside into the centre

gradually.

5. Line the base of the cake tin with silicone or lightly greased greaseproof paper.

6. Pour the gingerbread mixture into the cake tin, and bake in a preheated oven 160°C/325°F/Gas Mark 3, for 1-1½ hours, testing during this time with a skewer; which should come out clean when the cake is cooked.

7. Allow the cake to cool in the tin, before turning out onto a wire rack.

Cook's Notes

Time
Preparation takes about 15 minutes, cooking takes 1-1½ hours.

Variation
Add 60g/2oz chopped mixed fruit to the gingerbread mixture along with the spices.

Serving Idea
Serve as a dessert with a lemon sauce.

Freezing
This cake freezes well for up to 1 month.

VITAMIN
RICH

Introduction

Vitamins are substances that are vital to the maintenance of our bodies, yet so much is written concerning these invisible, potent elements in our food that few of us can tell fact from fiction.

There are many different vitamins, but we only need each in very small quantities, and if we maintain a well balanced and varied diet, the food we eat will generally provide us with more than enough vitamins for our daily needs. In certain circumstances, however, such as during pregnancy, illness or in old age, vitamin supplements may be required, and in these cases professional advice should be sought.

Vitamins are mainly identified by letter, but this in no way indicates their order of importance. In the case of vitamin B, there are several complex variations of vitamins within the one heading, and this is called the 'B complex'. The table below gives general guidance on some of the main vitamins, their source and function.

VITAMIN	SOURCE	FUNCTION
A	Oily fish, fats, offal, carrots, green vegetables, tomatoes, watercress	General growth, good eyesight, healthy skin
B.1	Yeast extract, wheatgerm, peanuts, wholemeal bread, eggs, pulses	Assists the nervous system and metabolism. Is water soluble and therefore easily lost in cooking
B.2	Milk, dairy products, almonds, mushrooms, pulses, red meat, green vegetables	Assists the metabolism and maintains health of mouth, lips and skin
B.3	Milk, eggs, yeast extract, red meat, dried apricots	Essential to the nervous system
B.6	Yeast, whole cereal products, offal, dairy products, bananas, leaf vegetables	Helps production of new cells and promotes nervous health
B.12	Offal, meat, eggs, cheese, milk	Assists the production of red blood cells
C	Fruit and vegetables	Helps the body resist infection, promotes good skin, helps absorption of iron
D	Oily fish, fats, dairy products, offal, red meat	Helps promote strong bones and teeth. Is produced in the body when there is exposure to sunlight
E	Whole cereal products, eggs, nuts, vegetable oil and wholemeal flour	Necessary for upkeep of blood cells, tissues and membranes
K	Widely available in many foods such as green vegetables, eggs and cereals	Helps blood to clot and assists in the healing of wounds

SERVES 6-8

COUNTRYSIDE TERRINE

This impressive terrine looks very professional yet is simple to make.

450g/1lb pig liver, minced
340g/12oz lean pork, minced
225g/8oz pork sausagemeat
1 clove garlic, crushed
2 shallots, finely chopped
45ml/3 tbsps Cognac
2.5ml/½ tsp ground allspice
Salt and freshly ground black pepper
5ml/1 tsp chopped fresh thyme or sage
225g/8oz streaky bacon, rind and any bones removed
30ml/2 tbsps double cream
120g/4oz smoked tongue or ham, cut into 6mm/¼-inch cubes
1 large bay leaf

1. Preheat oven to 180°C/350°F/Gas Mark 4.

2. In a large bowl, mix together the minced liver and pork, sausagemeat, garlic, shallots, Cognac, allspice, salt, pepper, and thyme. Stir with a wooden spoon until the ingredients are evenly mixed, but still coarse in texture.

3. Lay the strips of bacon on a flat surface and stretch them with the back of a knife.

4. Line a 900g/2lb loaf dish evenly with the strips of bacon, overlapping each strip slightly to avoid any of the terrine mixture pushing through during cooking.

5. Add the cream, cubed tongue and ham to the liver and pork mixture, blending with your hands to keep the texture coarse.

6. Press the terrine mixture into the bacon-lined loaf dish, spreading it evenly, and pushing down lightly to remove any air bubbles.

7. Place the bay leaf on the top and fold over any overlapping edges of bacon.

8. Cover the dish with a tight-fitting lid or two layers of aluminium foil.

9. Stand the loaf dish in a roasting tin and pour enough water around it to come halfway up the sides of the dish.

10. Bake the terrine for 2 hours, or until the juices run clear when a knife is inserted into the centre.

11. Remove the lid or foil and replace this with some fresh foil.

12. Weigh down the terrine with cans of food or balance scale weights. Allow the terrine to cool at room temperature, then refrigerate it overnight if possible, still weighted, until it is completely chilled and firm.

13. To serve, remove the weights and foil and carefully turn the terrine out onto a serving plate. Scrape away any fat or jelly that may be on the outside of the terrine, and cut into slices just before serving.

Step 4 Line a 900g/2lb loaf tin evenly with the strips of bacon, overlapping each strip slightly.

Step 12 Cover the terrine with a double thickness of fresh foil and weight it down with cans or scale weights.

Cook's Notes

Time
Preparation takes about 25 minutes, plus refrigeration time. Cooking takes approximately 2 hours.

Freezing
This recipe will freeze well for up to 3 months. It should be packed in plastic wrap and not aluminium or metal foil.

Vitamin Content
This recipe is an extremely good source of all the B complex vitamins.

SERVES 4
WATERCRESS SOUP

Watercress is packed with vitamins A, C and K, and makes delicious soup.

60g/2oz butter
1 leek, cleaned and thinly sliced
225g/8oz potatoes, peeled and sliced thinly
570ml/1 pint chicken stock
Pinch grated nutmeg
Salt and freshly ground black pepper
4 good bunches of watercress, washed and trimmed
45ml/3 tbsps cream
Few extra sprigs of watercress for garnish

1. Melt the butter in a large saucepan and gently cook the leek until it is just soft, stirring frequently to prevent it from browning.

2. Add the potatoes, stock, nutmeg and seasoning to the saucepan. Bring to the boil, then cover and simmer for 15 minutes.

3. Add the watercress and simmer for a further 10 minutes.

4. Cool the soup slightly, then using a food processor or blender, process until the vegetables are very finely chopped. Rinse the saucepan and stand a fine meshed sieve over the cleaned pan.

5. Push the puréed soup through the sieve using the back of a wooden spoon, working the watercress and vegetables through the mesh until only the tough stalks remain and the soup in the pan is a fine purée.

6. Adjust the seasoning and stir the cream into the soup. Reheat gently, taking care not to boil it. Serve garnished with the reserved watercress sprigs and a little cream if desired.

Step 1 Slowly soften the leek in the melted butter, stirring to prevent it from browning.

Step 4 Blend the soup in a food processor or liquidiser until the vegetables are very finely chopped.

Step 5 Push the soup through a fine meshed sieve using a wooden spoon, work the vegetable pulp through until only the tough stalks remain in the sieve.

Cook's Notes

Time
Preparation takes 15 minutes, cooking takes about 45 minutes.

Serving Idea
Chill the soup, and serve on a bed of crushed ice for a delicious variation.

Vitamin Content
Watercress is an excellent source of vitamins A, C and K.

SERVES 4

GAZPACHO

Gazpacho is a typically Spanish soup which is served well chilled,
accompanied by a selection of fresh vegetables.

450g/1lb ripe tomatoes
1 onion, peeled and chopped
1 green pepper, seeded and diced
½ cucumber, chopped
30ml/2 tbsps stale white breadcrumbs
2 cloves garlic, crushed
30ml/2 tbsps red wine vinegar
570ml/1 pint tomato juice
Salt and freshly ground black pepper

Accompaniments
½ cucumber, diced
10 spring onions, chopped
225g/8oz tomatoes, skinned, seeded and chopped
1 large green pepper, seeded and diced

1. Cut a small cross in the top of each of the ripe tomatoes, and plunge into a bowl of boiling water for a few seconds.

2. Carefully peel the skin away from the blanched tomatoes. Discard the skin and roughly chop the tomatoes, removing the tough stalk as you do.

3. Put the roughly chopped tomatoes into a liquidiser or food processor, along with the onion, pepper and cucumber. Blend until finely chopped.

4. Put the chopped vegetables into a bowl with the breadcrumbs, garlic, vinegar and tomato juice. Mix well to blend evenly and allow to stand for 15 minutes.

5. Season the tomato soup thoroughly, then push through a fine meshed sieve using the back of a wooden spoon and working well to press all the vegetables through, but keeping the pips out of the resulting purée.

6. Chill the soup well before serving, surrounded by bowls containing the accompaniments.

Step 2 Carefully peel the skin away from the blanched tomatoes using a sharp knife.

Step 5 Push the puréed vegetables through a nylon sieve using the back of a wooden spoon, working until all the pulp has been pressed through and the tomato pips remain.

Cook's Notes

Time
Preparation takes approximately 20 minutes, plus chilling time.

Serving Idea
Serve the individual bowls of soup on crushed ice.

Freezing
This soup is ideal for freezing.

Vitamin Content
Extremely high in vitamin C and the tomatoes are a good source of vitamin A.

SERVES 4-6

SPINACH GNOCCHI

Gnocchi are delicious spinach and cheese dumplings which can be served as a healthy starter or snack.

120g/4oz chopped, frozen spinach
225g/8oz ricotta cheese, crumbled
90g/3oz Parmesan cheese, finely grated
Salt and freshly ground pepper
Pinch freshly grated nutmeg
1 egg, lightly beaten
45g/3 tbsps butter

1. Defrost the spinach and press it between two plates to extract all the moisture.

Step 1 Press the spinach between two plates to remove excess moisture

2. Mix the spinach with the ricotta cheese, half the Parmesan cheese, the salt, pepper and nutmeg. Gradually add the egg, beating well until the mixture holds together when shaped.

3. With floured hands, shape the mixture into oval shapes. Use about 15ml/1 tbsp mixture for each gnocchi.

4. Lower into simmering water 3 or 4 at a time and allow to cook gently until the gnocchi float to the surface (about 1-2 minutes).

5. Remove with a draining spoon and place in a well buttered ovenproof dish.

6. When all the gnocchi are cooked, sprinkle on the re-

Step 3 Shape the gnocchi mixture with well-floured hands into ovals or balls.

Step 4 The gnocchi will float to the surface of the water when cooked. Remove with a draining spoon.

maining Parmesan cheese and dot with the remaining butter.

7. Reheat for 10 minutes in a hot oven and brown under a preheated grill before serving.

Cook's Notes

Time
Preparation takes 15 minutes, cooking takes about 20 minutes.

Variation
Accompany with a tomato or cheese sauce and a salad for a light meal.

Vitamin Content
Spinach is a good source of vitamin A and the cheese provides vitamin B.

SERVES 4

COURGETTE SALAD

Raw vegetables are full of vitamins, and courgette in particular has a delicious taste and texture.

225g/8oz macaroni
4 tomatoes
4-5 courgettes, sliced thinly
8 stuffed green olives, sliced
90ml/6 tbsps French dressing

1. Put the macaroni into a large saucepan and cover with boiling water. Add a little salt and simmer for 10 minutes, or until tender but still firm. Rinse in cold water and drain well.

2. Cut a small cross in the tops of each tomato and plunge into boiling water for 30 seconds.

3. Carefully remove the skins from the blanched tomatoes, using a sharp knife. Chop the tomatoes coarsely.

4. Mix all the ingredients in a large bowl and chill in the refrigerator for 30 minutes before serving.

Step 1 Rinse the macaroni in lots of cold water, then drain well forking it occasionally to prevent it sticking together.

Step 4 Mix all the ingredients together well, stirring thoroughly to blend the dressing in evenly.

Cook's Notes

Time
Preparation takes 15 minutes, cooking takes approximately 10 minutes.

Variation
Use any other pasta shape of your choice.

Preparation
If you prefer, the courgettes can be blanched in boiling water for 1 minute, then drained and cooled before mixing with the salad ingredients.

Vitamin Content
This recipe is high in vitamin C from the courgettes and tomatoes, vitamin A from the tomatoes and vitamin B from the pasta.

SERVES 4-6

WATERCRESS AND ORANGE SALAD

This colourful salad combination is ideal served with cold meats or fish.

3 large bunches of watercress
4 oranges
90ml/6 tbsps vegetable oil
Juice and rind of 1 orange
Pinch sugar
5ml/1 tsp lemon juice
Salt and freshly ground black pepper

1. Wash the watercress and carefully cut away any thick stalks. Break the watercress into small sprigs, discarding any yellow leaves.
2. Carefully remove the peel and pith from the oranges using a sharp knife. Catch any juice that spills in a small bowl.
3. Cutting carefully, remove the fleshy segments from between the thin membrane inside the orange. Squeeze any juice from the orange membrane into the bowl with the juice from the peel.

4. Arrange the watercress with the orange segments on a serving dish.

5. Put the remaining ingredients into the bowl with the reserved orange juice, and mix together well.

6. Pour the salad dressing over the oranges and watercress just before serving, to prevent the watercress from going limp.

Step 2 Carefully peel the oranges using a sharp knife, and collecting any juices in a small bowl.

Step 1 Break the watercress into small sprigs, discarding any yellow leaves as you go.

Step 3 Cut the orange segments carefully from between the inner membranes using a sharp knife.

Cook's Notes

Time
Preparation takes approximately 20 minutes.

Serving Idea
Serve this salad on a bed of finely grated carrot.

Variation
Use grapefruit instead of the oranges, and chicory instead of the watercress.

Vitamin Content
This salad is extremely high in vitamin C, and if served with carrot is also a good source of vitamin A.

SERVES 4

CHEESE SALAD

This cheese salad is distinctly Greek in origin, and is ideal as a starter as well as being substantial enough to serve as a light lunch.

½ small head of endive or Crisp lettuce
½ small Iceberg lettuce
1 small cucumber
4 large tomatoes
8-10 pitted green or black olives, halved
1 medium-sized Spanish or red onion, peeled and sliced
125g/4oz feta cheese
75ml/5 tbsps olive oil
30ml/2 tbsps red wine vinegar
5ml/1 tsp chopped fresh oregano
2.5ml/½ tsp freshly ground sea salt
1.25ml/¼ tsp freshly ground black pepper
2.5ml/½ tsp ready made German mustard

1. Wash the endive and lettuce leaves thoroughly. Pat them dry with kitchen paper and tear into bite-sized pieces.

2. Thinly slice the cucumber, peeling it if you wish.

3. Cut a small cross into the top of each tomato and plunge into boiling water for 30 seconds.

4. Carefully peel the skins from the blanched tomatoes and slice the flesh crosswise.

5. Put the endive, lettuce, cucumber, tomatoes, olives and onion into a serving bowl and toss them together until well mixed.

6. Cut the feta cheese into 1cm/½-inch cubes. Sprinkle

Step 1 Tear the lettuce and endive into pieces to prevent excessive bruising and destruction of vitamins in the leaves.

Step 4 Using a sharp knife, slice the peeled tomatoes crosswise.

these cubes over the salad in the serving bowl.

7. Put all the remaining ingredients into a small bowl and whisk together using a fork or small whisk.

8. Pour the dressing over the salad and serve immediately.

Cook's Notes

Time
Preparation takes 10-12 minutes.

Serving Idea
Serve with jacket potatoes or crusty French bread.

Variation
Use Cheddar or Cheshire cheese in place of the feta cheese.

V **Vitamin Content**
Leaf vegetables such as lettuce are an excellent source of vitamin K. The tomatoes and cucumber are high in vitamin C and the cheese is a good source of vitamins B and D.

SERVES 6

ROGNONS À LA DIJONNAISE

This delicious French dish makes good use of vitamin-rich kidneys, an offal which is often very underused in cookery.

750g/1½lbs lambs' kidneys
60g/2oz unsalted butter
1-2 shallots, finely chopped
280ml/½ pint dry white wine
90g/3oz lightly salted butter, softened
45ml/3 tbsps Dijon mustard
Salt, black pepper and lemon juice, to taste
30ml/2 tbsps chopped parsley

Step 2 Trim away any hard core from the centre of each kidney half using a small pair of sharp scissors.

Step 1 Trim the fat from each kidney and cut them in half lengthways.

Step 8 Whisk the butter, mustard, salt, pepper and lemon juice into the reduced sauce using a fork or small whisk and beating until it is thick.

1. Trim away any fat from the kidneys and slice them in half lengthways.

2. Carefully snip out any hard core from the centre using a pair of sharp scissors.

3. Melt the unsalted butter in a large frying pan and gently sauté the kidneys, uncovered, until they are light brown on all sides.

4. Remove the kidneys from the frying pan and keep them warm.

5. Add the shallots to the meat juices in the pan and cook

for about 1 minute, stirring frequently until they are just soft.

6. Add the wine and bring to the boil, stirring constantly and scraping the pan to remove any browned juices.

7. Boil this sauce rapidly for 3-4 minutes to reduce by about half. Remove the pan from the heat.

8. Put the softened butter into the pan with the mustard and seasonings. Whisk the mixture into the reduced sauce with a small whisk or fork.

9. Return the pan to the heat and add the kidneys and the parsley. Heat very gently for 1-2 minutes, taking care not to boil the mixture any further. Serve immediately.

Cook's Notes

Time
Preparation takes approximately 25 minutes, cooking takes 15-17 minutes.

Watchpoint
Do not overcook the kidneys or they will become tough.

Vitamin Content
Kidneys are an excellent source of vitamins A, B and D.

SERVES 6

PORK PROVENÇALE

This hearty casserole of lean pork topped with potatoes is suitable for serving as a family meal, or as part of a dinner party menu.

1 kg/2lbs pork fillets
60g/2oz butter
350g/12oz onions, peeled and thinly sliced
425g/15oz tin tomatoes
Salt and freshly ground black pepper
1.25ml/¼ tsp dried mixed herbs
750g/1½lbs potatoes, peeled and thinly sliced
15ml/1 tbsp chopped parsley for garnish

1. Trim the pork of any surplus fat and slice into thin strips.

2. Melt half of the butter in a large sauté pan and gently fry

Step 1 Slice the pork into thin strips using a sharp knife.

Step 4 Gently fry the onions in the meat juices until they are just soft.

the slices of meat, stirring continuously to prevent them from burning.

3. Transfer the meat to a plate and set aside.

4. Stir the onions into the meat juices in the sauté pan and cook gently until just soft.

5. Add the tomatoes to the pan along with the salt, pepper and mixed herbs. Bring to the boil, then simmer gently for about 5 minutes, or until the sauce has reduced by about a third.

6. Arrange the meat, sauce and potatoes in layers in an ovenproof serving dish, finishing with a layer of potato.

7. Melt the remaining butter and brush the top layer of potato with this.

8. Cover the dish with a lid or foil, and cook in the oven for 1½ hours at 180°C/350°F/Gas Mark 4.

9. Remove the lid from the dish and continue cooking for a further 30 minutes to brown the potatoes. Sprinkle with chopped parsley before serving.

Step 6 Arrange the meat, tomato sauce and potatoes in layers in an ovenproof serving dish.

Cook's Notes

Time
Preparation takes 25 minutes, cooking takes approximately 2 hours.

Freezing
This dish will freeze very well for up to 3 months. Freeze it before the final 30 minutes cooking time, then reheat by thawing and cooking uncovered for 1 hour at 180°C/350°F/Gas Mark 4.

Vitamin Content
The vegetables are a good source of vitamin C, and the tomatoes also contain vitamin A.

SERVES 4

LENTIL KEDGEREE

This delicious recipe combines spiced rice with lentils and onion to make a substantial vegetarian lunch or supper dish.

225g/8oz basmati rice
225g/8oz red lentils
750ml/1¼ pints warm water
120g/4oz butter, or olive oil
1 medium-sized onion, peeled and chopped
2.5ml/½ tsp crushed fresh root ginger
2.5ml/½ tsp crushed garlic
2.5cm/1-inch piece cinnamon stick
6 cloves
1 bay leaf
5ml/1 tsp ground coriander
1.25ml/¼ tsp ground turmeric
2.5ml/½ tsp freshly ground sea salt
2 green chillies, sliced in half lengthways

Step 5 Stir-fry the rice and lentils together, making sure that they are evenly coated with the fat.

1. Wash the rice and the lentils thoroughly in cold water. Drain well.

2. Put the drained rice and lentils into a large bowl and cover with the warm water. Soak for 30 minutes, then drain very thoroughly, reserving the water.

3. Heat the butter or olive oil in a large saucepan. Stir in the onion and fry gently for 2-3 minutes, stirring to prevent from burning.

4. Add the ginger, garlic, cinnamon stick, cloves and bay leaf to the onion and continue frying for 1 minute.

5. Add the rice and lentils to the fried onion, along with the coriander, turmeric, salt and green chilli. Stir over the heat for 2-3 minutes, until the rice and lentils are evenly coated

Step 6 Cook the rice and lentils until all the liquid has been absorbed, then fluff up with a fork before serving.

with fat.

6. Pour the reserved water into the rice mixture and bring to the boil. Reduce the heat and cover the pan with a tight fitting lid. Simmer for 8-10 minutes without stirring, or until the water has been completely absorbed.

7. Stir the rice and lentils together, remove and discard the chillies, and serve immediately.

Cook's Notes

Time
Preparation takes 15 minutes, plus soaking time. Cooking takes approximately 30 minutes.

Watchpoint
Great care must be taken when using fresh chillies. If any of the juice gets into your mouth or eyes, rinse with lots of cold water.

V Vitamin Content
Lentils and rice are both excellent sources of vitamin B.

SERVES 4

LENTIL AND VEGETABLE CURRY

Lentils are a staple ingredient in Indian cookery. This delicious vegetable curry should be made using fresh spices for the best flavour.

225g/8oz whole green lentils
30ml/2 tbsps vegetable oil
5ml/1 tsp salt
2.5ml/½ tsp mustard seed, crushed
5ml/1 tsp ground coriander
2.5ml/½ tsp ground cumin
2 dried red chillies, crushed
1 carrot, peeled and sliced diagonally
1 potato, peeled and cubed
6-8 okra, topped and tailed, then cut into 2.5cm/1-inch
    pieces
1 small courgette, sliced diagonally
1 small aubergine, halved and sliced
375ml/¾ pint water
6 curry leaves
1 green chilli, slit in half and chopped
5ml/1 tsp fresh chopped mint
15ml/1 tbsp fresh chopped coriander
Coriander leaves for garnish

1. Wash the lentils in warm water until it runs clear. Drain well.

2. Put the lentils into a large saucepan and pour over 570ml/1 pint water. Simmer gently for 15-20 minutes.

3. When the lentils are soft, beat with a potato masher or whisk until they are puréed.

4. In a large saucepan heat the oil and gently fry the mustard seed, ground coriander, cumin and dried chillies for 1 minute.

5. Add the vegetables to the spices and cook for 2 minutes, stirring all the time, to coat them evenly in the oil and spice mixture.

6. Add the water and the puréed lentils to the vegetable mixture and stir well.

7. Add the curry leaves, chopped chilli, mint and fresh coriander, then cook for 15 minutes. Serve hot, garnished with coriander leaves.

Step 3 Using a potato masher or whisk, break up the cooked lentils until they are well puréed.

Step 6 Stir the puréed lentils into the vegetable mixture.

Cook's Notes

Time
Preparation takes about 10 minutes, cooking takes 20-30 minutes.

Variation
Use any combination of fresh vegetables to vary this curry.

Serving Idea
Serve with boiled basmati rice.

V **Vitamin Content**
Lentils provide an excellent source of vitamin B and fresh vegetables provide vitamins A and C.

SERVES 4

BEEF WITH PINEAPPLE AND PEPPERS

This delicious sweet and sour main course is distinctly Chinese in origin.

450g/1lb fillet or rump steak
1 small pineapple
1 green pepper
1 red pepper
15ml/1 tbsp peanut oil
1 onion, peeled and roughly chopped
2 cloves garlic, crushed
2.5cm/1-inch fresh root ginger, peeled and thinly sliced
5ml/1 tsp sesame oil
30ml/2 tbsps light soy sauce
15ml/1 tbsp dark soy sauce
5ml/1 tsp sugar
15ml/1 tbsp brown sauce
60ml/4 tbsps water
Salt and freshly ground black pepper

1. Using a sharp knife, cut the steak into thin strips.

2. Carefully peel the pineapple and cut out any eyes using a sharp knife or potato peeler. Cut the pineapple into slices and chop them into bite-sized pieces, removing the hard core.

3. Slice the green and red peppers in half. Remove and discard the cores and seeds. Chop the pepper flesh into thin strips.

4. Heat the peanut oil in a wok or large frying pan, and gently fry the onion, garlic and ginger, stirring continuously until the onion has softened slightly.

5. Add the strips of beef and the strips of pepper, and continue stir-frying for 3 minutes.

6. Add the pineapple and stir-fry again for 2 minutes.

7. Remove the meat, vegetables and fruit from the wok, and put on a plate. Set aside.

8. Stir the sesame oil into the juices in the wok and add the soy sauces, sugar, brown sauce and water. Simmer rapidly for 30 seconds to reduce and thicken.

9. Stir the fruit, vegetables and beef back into the sauce. Season, heat through and serve immediately.

Step 1 Using a sharp knife, cut the steak into thin strips.

Step 5 Stir-fry the beef and peppers with the onions in the wok.

Cook's Notes

Time
Preparation takes 30 minutes, cooking takes about 10 minutes.

Serving Idea
Serve with spring rolls and plain boiled rice.

Watchpoint
Take care not to overcook the meat and vegetables, as this will greatly reduce the vitamin content of this dish.

V Vitamin Content
Steak is an excellent source of vitamin B and the vegetables and fruit are high in vitamin C.

SERVES 4

KIDNEYS WITH BACON

Stir-frying is an excellent way of cooking kidneys, as the speedy cooking ensures that they do not become tough.

450g/1lb lambs' kidneys
30ml/2 tbsps vegetable oil
8 rashers lean bacon, cut into 2.5cm/1-inch strips
1 onion, peeled and chopped
3 cloves garlic, crushed
15ml/1 tbsp tomato chutney
15ml/1 tbsp light soy sauce
30ml/2 tbsps water
Salt and freshly ground black pepper
15ml/1 tbsp cornflour
45ml/3 tbsps sherry
22ml/1½ tbsps fresh chopped parsley

1. Trim the fat from the kidneys and cut each kidney in half with a sharp knife.

2. Carefully trim out the hard core from the centre of each kidney with a sharp knife or scissors.

3. Cut a lattice design on the back of each kidney using a sharp knife and taking care not to cut right through.

4. Put the kidneys into a bowl and stir in the sherry. Set aside for 15 minutes to marinate.

5. Heat the oil in a large wok and fry the bacon, onion and garlic for 5 minutes, stirring continuously to prevent burning. Remove from the wok and set aside on a plate.

6. Drain the kidneys and reserve the sherry marinade. Add the kidneys to the wok and stir for 3 minutes only.

7. Stir the tomato chutney, soy sauce and water into the wok with the kidneys, then add the bacon and onion mixture. Season with salt and pepper and stir-fry gently for 5 minutes.

8. Blend the cornflour with the sherry marinade.

9. Add 1 tbsp parsley to the cornflour mixture and stir this

Step 2 Remove the hard core from each kidney half using a sharp knife or a small pair of scissors.

Step 3 Cut a lattice design on the backs of each kidney, using a sharp knife, and taking care not to cut right through.

Step 6 Stir-fry the kidneys until they are completely browned.

into the kidneys in the wok, mixing well until the sauce is thickened and smooth. Serve at once, sprinkled with a little extra parsley.

 Cook's Notes

Time
Preparation takes 20 minutes, cooking takes 25 minutes.

Serving Idea
Serve with rice or creamed potatoes.

Vitamin Content
All offal is an excellent source of vitamins A, B and D.

SERVES 4

MONKFISH AND PEPPER KEBABS

Monkfish is ideal for making kebabs as it can be cut into firm cubes which do not disintegrate during cooking.

8 rashers of lean bacon, rind removed
450g/1lb monkfish, skinned and cut into 2.5cm/1-inch
  pieces
1 small green pepper, seeded and cut into 2.5cm/1-inch
  pieces
1 small red pepper, seeded and cut into 2.5cm/1-inch
  pieces
12 small mushroom caps
8 bay leaves
45ml/3 tbsps vegetable oil
120ml/4 fl oz dry white wine
60ml/4 tbsps tarragon vinegar
2 shallots, finely chopped
15ml/1 tbsp chopped fresh tarragon
15ml/1 tbsp chopped fresh chervil or parsley
225g/8oz butter, softened
Salt and freshly ground black pepper

1. Cut the bacon rashers in half lengthways and then again in half crosswise.

2. Put a piece of the fish onto each piece of bacon and roll the bacon around the piece of fish.

3. Thread the bacon and fish rolls onto large skewers, alternating them with slices of pepper, mushroom and the bay leaves.

4. Brush the kebabs with oil and arrange on a grill pan.

5. Preheat the grill to hot and cook the kebabs for 10-15 minutes, turning them frequently to prevent the kebabs from burning.

6. Heat the white wine, vinegar and shallots in a small

Step 2 Wrap each piece of fish in one of the strips of bacon.

Step 8 Add the butter gradually into the simmering wine, whisking briskly to thicken the sauce.

saucepan until boiling. Cook rapidly to reduce by half.

7. Add the herbs and lower the heat.

8. Using a fork or small whisk beat the butter bit by bit into the hot wine mixture, whisking rapidly until the sauce becomes thick. Season to taste.

9. Arrange the kebabs on a serving plate and serve with a little of the sauce spooned over and the remainder in a separate jug.

Cook's Notes

Time
Preparation takes 30 minutes, cooking will take about 25 minutes.

Preparation
When making the sauce it is important to whisk briskly, or it will not thicken sufficiently.

Vitamin Content
Fish is an excellent source of vitamins A and D. Bacon is a good source of vitamin B, and peppers are high in vitamin C.

SERVES 4

SWORDFISH STEAKS WITH GREEN PEPPERCORNS AND GARLIC SAUCE

Swordfish steaks are delicious and are now easily available at most good fishmongers.

30ml/2 tbsps fresh green peppercorns
90ml/6 tbsps lemon juice
60ml/4 tbsps olive oil
Freshly ground sea salt
4 swordfish steaks
1 egg
1 clove garlic, roughly chopped
140ml/¼ pint oil
30ml/2 tsps fresh oregano
Salt and freshly ground black pepper

1. Crush the green peppercorns lightly using a pestle and mortar.

2. Mix the lemon juice, olive oil and salt into the lightly crushed green peppercorns.

3. Place the swordfish steaks in a shallow ovenproof dish and pour the lemon and oil mixture over each steak. Re-frigerate overnight, turning occasionally until the fish becomes opaque.

4. Using a blender or food processor, mix together the eggs and garlic.

5. With the machine still running, gradually pour the oil through the funnel in a thin steady stream onto the egg and garlic mixture. Continue to blend until the sauce is thick.

6. Remove the leaves from the oregano sprigs and chop them finely.

7. Preheat the grill to hot and arrange the swordfish on the grill pan.

8. Sprinkle the chopped oregano over the swordfish steaks and season well. Cook for 15 minutes, turning them frequently and basting with the lemon and pepper marinade.

9. When the steaks are cooked, place onto a serving dish and spoon the garlic mayonnaise over to serve.

Step 1 Lightly crush the green peppercorns using a pestle and mortar.

Step 3 Marinate the swordfish steaks overnight, after such time they should be opaque.

Cook's Notes

Time
Preparation takes 25 minutes, plus overnight soaking.
Cooking takes about 15 minutes.

Variation
Substitute 30ml/2 tbsps well rinsed canned green peppercorns in place of the fresh peppercorns if you cannot get these, and use tuna steaks instead of the swordfish if you prefer.

Serving Idea
Serve with jacket potatoes and fresh salad.

Vitamin Content
The fish contains vitamins B and D.

SERVES 4

TARRAGON GRILLED RED MULLET

Red mullet is a very decorative little fish that is now readily available at fishmongers and supermarkets.

4 large or 8 small red mullets, gutted, scaled, washed and dried
4 or 8 sprigs of fresh tarragon
60ml/4 tbsps vegetable oil
30ml/2 tbsps tarragon vinegar
Salt and freshly ground black pepper
1 egg
5ml/1 tsp Dijon mustard
120ml/4 fl oz sunflower oil
15ml/1 tbsp wine vinegar
5ml/1 tsp brandy
15ml/1 tbsp chopped fresh tarragon
15ml/1 tbsp chopped fresh parsley
15ml/1 tbsp double cream

1. Rub the inside of each mullet with a teaspoonful of salt, scrubbing hard to remove any discoloured membranes inside. Rinse thoroughly.

2. Place a sprig of fresh tarragon inside each fish.

3. Using a sharp knife cut 2 diagonal slits on the side of each fish.

4. Mix together the vegetable oil, tarragon vinegar and a little salt and pepper in a small bowl.

5. Arrange the fish on a shallow dish and pour over the tarragon, vinegar marinade, brushing some of the mixture into the cuts on the side of the fish. Refrigerate for 30 minutes.

6. Put the egg into a blender or food processor along with the mustard and a little salt and pepper. Process for 2-3 seconds to mix.

7. With the machine running, add the oil through the funnel in a thin steady stream. Continue blending the dressing until it is thick and creamy.

8. Add the vinegar, brandy and herbs, and process for a further 30 seconds to mix well.

9. Lightly whip the cream with a small whisk until it thickens.

10. Fold the slightly thickened cream carefully into the oil and vinegar dressing. Pour into a serving dish and refrigerate until ready to use.

11. Arrange the fish on a grill pan and cook under a pre-heated hot grill for 5-8 minutes per side, depending on the size of the fish. Baste frequently with the marinade while cooking, then serve with a little of the sauce and some sprigs of fresh tarragon, if you like.

Step 1 Rub the insides of each fish with a teaspoonful of salt, scrubbing briskly to remove any discoloured membranes.

Step 3 Using a sharp knife, cut 2 diagonal slits on the side of each fish, taking great care not to cut right through the flesh.

Cook's Notes

Time
Preparation takes about 15 minutes, cooking takes 10-16 minutes.

Variation
Use herrings or mackerel in place of the mullet.

Vitamin Content
All fish is an excellent source of vitamins A and D.

SERVES 4

DUCK WITH ORANGES

This traditional combination is given extra flavour by cooking the duck in a distinctly oriental manner.

---

3 oranges
1 duck
15g/½oz butter
15ml/1 tbsp oil
280ml/½ pint light chicken stock
90ml/3 fl oz red wine
30ml/2 tbsps redcurrant jelly
Salt and freshly ground black pepper
5ml/1 tsp arrowroot
15ml/1 tbsp cold water

---

1. Using a potato peeler carefully pare the rind thinly off 2 of the oranges.

Step 2 Using a sharp knife carefully cut the parred orange rind into very thin strips.

2. Cut the rind into very fine shreds using a sharp knife. Put the shredded orange rind into a small bowl and cover with boiling water. Set aside to blanch for 5 minutes, then drain.

3. Squeeze the juice from the 2 oranges. Set this aside.

4. Cut away the peel and the pith from the remaining orange and then slice the flesh into thin rounds. Set aside.

5. Wash the duck and dry well with absorbent kitchen paper.

6. Put the butter and the oil into a large wok and heat until melted. Add the duck and fry, turning frequently until it is brown all over.

7. Remove the duck from the wok, cool slightly and using poultry shears, cut away the leg and wing ends. Cut the duck in half lengthways and then cut each half into 2.5cm/1-inch strips.

8. Remove the fat from the wok and return the duck to the wok. Add the stock, red wine, redcurrant jelly, squeezed orange juice, and the well drained strips of rind. Bring to the boil, then season to taste. Reduce the heat, cover the

Step 7 Cut each half of the duck into 2.5cm/1-inch strips using poultry shears or a very sharp knife.

wok and simmer the duck gently for 20 minutes, or until well cooked.

9. Skim away any surface fat and thicken the sauce by mixing the arrowroot with the water and stirring into the wok. Bring the mixture back to the boil and simmer for a further 5 minutes, or until the sauce is thick.

10. Arrange the duck on a serving plate and garnish with the orange slices and some additional watercress if liked.

Cook's Notes

Time
Preparation takes 30 minutes, cooking takes 35 minutes.

Serving Idea
Serve with plain boiled rice or sautéed potatoes.

Vitamin Content
Duck is a good source of vitamin B, and oranges are an excellent source of vitamin C.

SERVES 4-6
LIVER WITH ONIONS

This dish is simple to prepare, but absolutely delicious and highly nutritious.

450g/1lb onions
450g/1lb lambs' liver, thinly sliced
Salt and freshly ground black pepper
45g/1½oz plain flour
45ml/3 tbsps vegetable oil
30g/1 oz butter
30ml/2 tbsps fresh chopped parsley

1. Peel the onions and slice thinly, keeping each slice in

Step 1 Using a sharp knife, thinly slice the peeled onions, keeping them in rings if possible.

circles if possible.

2. Trim away any large pipes or tubes from the liver using a pair of small scissors or a sharp knife.

3. Mix the seasoning and the flour together on a plate and lay the slices of liver into the flour, turning them and pressing them gently to coat all over evenly.

4. Put the oil and the butter into a large frying pan. Heat

Step 2 Trim away any pipes or tubes from the liver slices using a small pair of scissors or a sharp knife

Step 3 Coat each liver slice thoroughly with the seasoned flour, pressing it gently onto the surface.

gently until foaming.

5. Add the onion rings and fry until just golden.

6. Add the liver slices and fry for 3-5 minutes on each side until well cooked. Cooking time will depend on the thickness of each slice.

7. Stir the parsley into the liver and onions and serve immediately on hot plates.

Cook's Notes

Time
Preparation takes 15 minutes, cooking takes about 10 minutes.

Variation
Add 120g/4oz shredded streaky bacon with the onions.

Serving Idea
Serve with creamed potatoes and green vegetables.

Watchpoint
Do not overcook liver or any offal, as it will toughen.

Freezing
Liver freezes well, but should be frozen before cooking.

Vitamin Content
Onions are a good source of vitamin C. Liver is an excellent source of vitamins A, B and D.

SERVES 4
RICE PUDDING

Rice pudding has always been a firm family favourite and this recipe adds spices to make it special enough even for dinner parties.

60g/2oz unsalted butter
1 bay leaf, crumbled
2.5cm/1-inch piece cinnamon stick, crushed
175g/6oz pudding rice, washed and drained
1.2 ltrs/2 pints milk
400ml/⅔ pint evaporated milk
175g/6oz granulated sugar
60g/2oz chopped blanched almonds
Seeds of 8 small cardamoms, crushed
30g/1oz pistachio nuts, chopped or cut into slivers

1. Melt the butter in a saucepan and fry the bay leaf and cinnamon for 1 minute.

2. Add the rice and stir well to coat evenly with the melted fat.

3. Add the milk and bring the mixture to the boil, then reduce the heat and simmer for 40-50 minutes, stirring occasionally to prevent the rice from sticking to the pan.

4. Add the sugar and the evaporated milk to the rice mixture and continue cooking for a further 20-30 minutes, stirring frequently to prevent burning.

5. It is important to keep stirring the mixture during this cooking time to bring up thin layers of light brown skin which form on the base of the saucepan. This is what gives the pudding its rich, reddish tinge and caramel flavour.

6. Add the chopped almonds and the crushed cardamom seeds to the rice puddings. Stir well and pour into a large serving dish.

7. Decorate the top of the rice pudding with the slivered pistachio nuts, and serve hot or cold.

Step 5 Stir the pudding frequently to bring up the thin layers of light brown skin which will form on the base of the saucepan during cooking.

Step 2 Stir the rice into the fried bay leaf and cinnamon, mixing well to coat each grain evenly with the flavoured fat.

Step 7 Decorate the pudding with slivered pistachios before serving.

Cook's Notes

Time
Preparation takes 10 minutes, cooking takes 1 hour 30 minutes.

! **Watchpoint**
Frequent stirring is important in this recipe to prevent the sugar from caramelising too much and giving a bitter flavour to the dessert.

V **Vitamin Content**
Rice contains vitamins from the B group, and milk and evaporated milk contain vitamins A and D.

SERVES 4-6

SUMMER PUDDING

This favourite summer dessert simply oozes vitamins and flavour.

750g/1½lbs fresh soft fruit, e.g. raspberries, strawberries, rhubarb, redcurrants, blackcurrants or any combination of these fruits
175g/6oz granulated sugar
10 thick slices of white bread, crusts removed
420ml/¾ pint fresh cream
450g/1lb fresh whole raspberries

1. Put the 1½lbs of mixed fruit into a large saucepan and stir in the sugar.

2. Heat the fruit gently, shaking the pan vigorously so that the sugar dissolves but the fruit stays as intact as possible. Remove from the heat and cool completely.

3. Cut the slices of bread into thick fingers and use them to line the base and sides of a 900 ml/1½ pint pudding basin. Press the slices of bread together as firmly as possible to avoid leaving any gaps between them.

4. Pour the cooled fruit and the juice into the centre of the pudding, and cover the top completely with the remaining bread. Press down firmly.

5. Place a saucer or small plate over the top of the pudding and weigh this down with cans of food or balance scale weights.

6. Chill the pudding overnight in the refrigerator.

7. Remove the weights and the small plate or saucer. Loosen the sides of the pudding carefully with a round bladed knife, and invert a serving plate over the top of the bowl.

8. Carefully turn both the serving plate and the bowl over, and shake gently. The pudding should drop onto the serving plate.

9. Whip the cream until it is thick, then spread approximately half of the cream over the summer pudding.

Step 2 Shake the fruit and sugar together gently over a low heat until the sugar dissolves, but the fruit remains mainly intact.

Step 3 Press the slices of bread together well around the sides and the base of the pudding dish, trying to make sure that there are no gaps in between each slice.

Step 10 Press the whole raspberries into the cream layer covering the summer pudding.

10. Press the fresh raspberries onto the cream in a thick layer all over the pudding, and pipe the remaining cream in small rosettes between the gaps.

11. Chill well, before serving.

Cook's Notes

 Time
Preparation takes approximately 30 minutes, plus overnight chilling.

Freezing
This pudding freezes extremely well, but should be decorated with the fruit and cream after it has been thawed.

V **Vitamin Content**
The bread contains vitamin B, the fruit contains vitamin C, and the cream contains vitamin D.

SERVES 4-6

CARROTELLA

Carrots have a natural sweetness which lends itself to sweet as well as savoury dishes. Carrotella is a sweet and spicy dessert which should be served very cold.

1.2 lts/2 pints milk
450g/1lb carrots, peeled and finely grated
190ml/⅓ pint evaporated milk
120g/4oz granulated sugar
60g/2oz sultanas
Seeds of 8 small cardamoms, crushed
2 drops vanilla essence
30g/1oz chopped blanched almonds
30g/1oz chopped pistachio nuts

1. Put the milk into a saucepan and simmer over a low heat until reduced to about 850ml/1½ pints.

2. Add the carrots. Cover and cook over a medium heat for approximately 15 minutes, or until the carrots have begun to soften.

3. Stir in the evaporated milk, sugar and sultanas, re-cover and simmer gently for about another 5 minutes.

4. Remove the saucepan from the heat, then stir in the crushed cardamom seed and vanilla essence.

5. Beat the carrotella briskly to break up the carrots, then turn into a serving dish and cool slightly.

6. Sprinkle the nuts on top and chill very well before serving.

Step 2 Cook the carrots over a medium heat for 15 minutes, or until they have softened and are breaking up.

Step 6 Sprinkle the partially chilled carrotella with the chopped and flaked nuts.

Cook's Notes

Time
Preparation takes 15 minutes. Cooking takes 40 minutes, plus chilling time.

Serving Idea
Serve with a spoonful of chilled fromage frais.

Variation
Use rosewater instead of the vanilla essence, and finely chopped hazelnuts instead of the pistachio nuts.

Vitamin Content
Milk and evaporated milk contain vitamins D and E. Carrots are an excellent source of vitamins A and C.

SERVES 4

BROWN BREAD ICE CREAM

This unusual ice cream is easy to make and is an ideal standby dessert to keep in the freezer.

2 egg yolks
60g/2oz caster sugar
450ml/¾ pint double, or whipping cream
Few drops of vanilla essence
240ml/8 fl oz water
180g/6oz soft brown sugar
90ml/6 tbsps fresh brown breadcrumbs
5ml/1 tsp ground cinnamon

1. Put the egg yolks and the caster sugar into a bowl, and whisk vigorously with an electric beater until thick, pale and creamy.

2. Pour in the double cream and continue whisking until thick and creamy.

3. Beat in the vanilla essence, then pour the cream mixture into a freezer-proof container and freeze for 1 hour, or until beginning to set around the edges.

4. Break the ice cream away from the edges and whisk with the electric beater until the ice crystals have broken. Return to the freezer and chill for a further hour. Repeat this procedure 2 more times, then freeze completely.

5. Put the water and the brown sugar into a small saucepan and heat gently, stirring until the sugar has dissolved. Bring the mixture to the boil and boil rapidly until the sugar caramelises.

6. Remove the caramel sugar from the heat and stir in the breadcrumbs and the cinnamon.

7. Spread the caramel mixture onto a baking sheet lined with oiled greaseproof paper, and allow to set.

8. Break up the caramelised breadcrumbs by placing

Step 1 Whisk the eggs and caster sugar together until they are pale, thick and creamy.

Step 7 When cooled, the caramelised breadcrumbs should set completely hard.

them in plastic food bags and crushing with a rolling pin.

9. Turn the frozen ice cream into a large bowl and break it up with a fork.

10. Allow the ice cream to soften slightly, then stir in the caramelised breadcrumbs, mixing thoroughly to blend evenly.

11. Return the brown bread ice cream to the freezer tray and freeze completely.

12. Allow the mixture to soften for 10 minutes before serving in scoops with a crisp biscuit.

Cook's Notes

Time
Preparation takes approximately 40 minutes, plus freezing time.

Preparation
Be very careful when making the caramel sugar as it can burn very easily.

Vitamin Content
Wholemeal bread contains vitamins B and E. Fresh cream contains vitamins A, B and D.

SERVES 4-6
FRUITY BREAD PUDDING

This traditional family pudding is made extra nutritious by using wholemeal
bread and a rich assortment of dried fruits.

120g/4oz raisins
120g/4oz currants
120g/4oz sultanas
120g/4oz prunes, stoned and chopped
Finely grated rind and juice of 1 orange
8 thick slices wholemeal bread, crusts removed
60g/2oz butter, softened
120g/4oz soft brown sugar
280ml/½ pint whole milk
2 eggs, lightly beaten
1.25ml/¼ tsp ground nutmeg
1.25ml/¼ tsp ground cinnamon

1. Put all the dried fruit, orange rind and orange juice into a large bowl and mix well.

2. Put about half of the mixed fruit into the base of a lightly buttered ovenproof serving dish.

3. Spread the bread with the butter and cut it into small squares.

4. Arrange half of the bread squares over the fruit in the base of the serving dish.

5. Sprinkle with half of the brown sugar, then repeat the layers once again, finishing with a layer of sugar.

6. Whisk together the milk, eggs, nutmeg and cinnamon. Pour the mixture over the bread pudding and allow to stand for 1 hour.

7. Bake the pudding in a preheated oven, 190°C/375°F/ Gas Mark 5, for about 35-40 minutes, or until crisp on top but still soft at the bottom. Serve very hot.

Step 5 Arrange the fruit, bread and sugar in layers in an ovenproof dish.

Step 3 Cut the buttered bread into squares approximately 5cm/2 inches.

Step 6 Pour the egg and milk mixture over the bread and fruit, taking care not to dislodge the pieces of bread.

Cook's Notes

Time
Preparation takes 15 minutes, plus 1 hour soaking. Cooking takes 40 minutes.

Freezing
This pudding will freeze well and should be reheated for 20 minutes in a hot oven, 190°C/375°F/ Gas Mark 5. Cover the top with foil to prevent it from burning or browning further.

Vitamin Content
Dried fruit is an excellent source of vitamin C, and milk and eggs are good sources of vitamins A, B, D and E. Wholemeal bread is an excellent source of vitamins B and E.

SERVES 4

CARAMEL ORANGES

Rich in vitamins A and C, oranges need very little preparation to provide a delicious dessert.

4 large oranges
280g/10oz granulated sugar
340ml/12 fl oz water
60ml/2 fl oz boiling water
30ml/2 tbsps Cointreau

1. Using a potato peeler or very sharp knife, carefully pare the peel only from the oranges. Cut this peel into very thin strips, removing any white pith as you do so.

2. Put the orange peel strips into a small bowl and cover with boiling water. Allow to stand for 20 minutes, then drain.

3. Carefully peel all the pith from the oranges with a serrated edged knife. Cut the oranges horizontally into slices approximately 5ml/¼-inch thick. Reserve any juice which spills in a small jug.

4. Put the orange juice, the 340ml/12 fl oz water and sugar into a small saucepan, and heat gently all the time until the sugar has dissolved.

5. Increase the temperature and bring the sugar syrup to the boil, boiling rapidly until it turns a pale gold colour.

6. Remove the caramel from the heat and quickly stir in the 60ml/2 fl oz of boiling water.

7. Add the orange rind to the sugar syrup along with the Cointreau, and allow to cool completely.

8. Arrange the orange slices in a serving dish, and pour over the cooled syrup. Chill for several hours or overnight, before serving.

Step 1 Cut the parred orange rind into very thin julienne strips with a sharp knife.

Step 3 Carefully remove all the white pith from the oranges, using a serrated knife and cutting with a sawing action.

Step 5 Cook the sugar and the syrup over a moderate heat, until it turns pale gold in colour. Take care not to overcook at this stage.

Cook's Notes

Time
Preparation takes 25 minutes, cooking takes 20 minutes.

Watchpoint
Take care not to overcook the sugar syrup or it will burn and spoil the flavour.

Preparation
Hold the pan slightly away from you when adding the boiling water, as the syrup will splutter and spit and can give a very nasty burn.

Freezing
Fresh oranges freeze very well, but sugar syrup should be made fresh each time.

Vitamin Content
Oranges are an excellent source of vitamins A and C.

MAKES 1 x 25cm/10-INCH LOAF

CARROT CAKE

Carrots give a cake a delicious sweet flavour, as well as lots of vitamins and minerals. What better excuse do you need to indulge in this delicious tea-time treat.

175g/6oz butter
175g/6oz soft brown sugar
2 eggs, well beaten
225g/8oz plain wholemeal flour
7.5ml/1½ tsps bicarbonate of soda
2.5ml/½ tsp baking powder
1.25ml/¼ tsp ground cinnamon
1.25ml/¼ tsp ground nutmeg
2.5ml/½ tsp salt
225g/8oz peeled carrots, grated
90g/3oz raisins
60g/2oz finely chopped walnuts
1.25ml/¼ tsp cardamom seeds, crushed
Icing sugar, for dredging

1. Cream the butter and sugar together until they are light and fluffy.

2. Add the eggs a little at a time, beating well and adding a teaspoonful of the flour with each addition, to prevent the mixture from curdling.

3. Put the remaining flour into a large bowl along with the bicarbonate of soda, baking powder, cinnamon, nutmeg and salt. Mix together well.

4. Carefully fold the flour into the butter and egg mixture, mixing well to ensure that it is blended evenly.

5. Add the carrots, raisins, nuts and cardamom seeds, beating the mixture well to blend evenly.

6. Lightly grease a 25cm/10-inch loaf tin and line the base with a piece of silicone paper.

7. Pour the cake mixture into the loaf tin, and bake in a preheated oven 180°C/350°F/Gas Mark 4, for 45-50 minutes or until a fine metal skewer comes out clean when inserted into the centre of the cake.

8. Cool the cake in its tin for 15 minutes before turning out onto a wire rack to cool completely.

9. Dredge the cake with icing sugar just before serving.

Step 2 Beat the eggs gradually into the butter and sugar, adding a little flour with each addition to prevent the mixture from curdling.

Step 5 Stir the carrots, fruit and nuts into the cake mixture, mixing well to blend evenly.

Cook's Notes

 Time
Preparation takes 30 minutes, cooking takes 45-50 minutes.

! **Watchpoint**
If the egg and butter mixture should curdle, add a little more flour and beat very hard with an electric whisk until the curdling disappears.

V **Vitamin Content**
Wholemeal flour is an excellent source of vitamins B and D. Carrots are an excellent source of vitamins A and C.

MAKES 1 x 20cm/8-INCH CAKE

TOASTED ALMOND CAKE

A crunchy toasted almond topping makes this cake very different from run-of-the-mill tea-time treats.

150g/5oz butter, softened
90g/3oz caster sugar
2 eggs, lightly beaten
180g/6oz wholemeal self-raising flour
2.5ml/½ tsp vanilla essence
30ml/2 tbsps orange juice
60g/2oz soft brown sugar
60ml/4 tbsps melted, unsalted, butter
15ml/1 tbsp milk
60g/2oz flaked almonds
60g/2oz icing sugar
30ml/2 tbsps cornflour
3 egg yolks
140ml/¼ pint milk
90ml/3 fl oz double cream, whipped
1.25ml/¼ tsp almond essence

---

1. Cream the butter and caster sugar until it is light and fluffy.

2. Beat in the eggs one at a time, adding a teaspoonful of the flour with each addition to prevent the mixture from curdling.

3. Fold in all the remaining flour, along with the vanilla essence and the orange juice.

4. Lightly grease a 20cm/8-inch cake tin, and line the base with a piece of silicone paper.

5. Spoon the cake mixture into the tin and spread the top evenly with a palette knife.

6. Put the brown sugar into a small saucepan, along with the melted butter, the 15ml/1 tbsp milk and the flaked almonds. Stir over a low heat until the sugar has completely dissolved.

7. Sprinkle about 15ml/1 tbsp of additional flour over the top of the cake mixture in the tin, then pour over the melted sugar, butter and almond mixture. Spread it evenly, but try not to disturb the cake mixture too much.

8. Bake the cake in a preheated oven 190°C/375°F/Gas Mark 5 for 20-30 minutes, or until the cake is well risen and the topping has caramelised golden brown.

9. Put the icing sugar, cornflour and egg yolks into a bowl, and using an electric beater, whisk until they are light and fluffy.

10. Pour on the milk, gradually whisking between additions. Strain this egg yolk mixture through a sieve into a heavy-based saucepan.

11. Cook the egg yolk and milk mixture over a gentle heat until it begins to thicken, and will thickly coat the back of a wooden spoon. Stir the mixture frequently during the cooking time to prevent it from burning or curdling.

12. Remove from the heat and cool.

13. When the custard is completely cool, lightly fold in the cream and the almond essence.

14. When the cake has cooled, carefully cut it in half horizontally with a sharp knife. Sandwich the two halves back together using the almond custard as a filling.

15. Chill thoroughly before serving.

Cook's Notes

Time
Preparation takes 40 minutes. Cooking takes about 30 minutes, plus 10 minutes for the filling.

Watchpoint
Do not allow the flaked almond topping to become too hot. Heat it just long enough to dissolve the sugar. If it does overheat, allow it to cool before pouring onto the uncooked cake mixture.

Vitamin Content
Wholemeal flour contains B group vitamins and vitamin E. Nuts contain vitamins B and E, and butter and eggs contain vitamins A, B, D and E. Milk and cream contain vitamins A and D.

MAKES 1 x 20cm/8-INCH CAKE

CINNAMON BUTTER CREAM CAKE

This sumptuous cake has the added advantage of requiring no cooking.

280g/10oz granulated sugar
2.5ml/½ tsp ground cinnamon
90ml/6 tbsps water
8 egg yolks
450g/1lb unsalted butter, softened
48 sponge fingers
120ml/8 tbsps brandy
120g/4oz toasted almonds, roughly chopped
120g/4oz plain chocolate, coarsely grated

Step 9 Line the cake tin with trimmed sponge biscuits spread with approximately half of the butter cream.

1. Put the sugar, water and cinnamon in a small heavy-based saucepan and bring to the boil, stirring constantly until the sugar dissolves.

2. Allow the sugar syrup to boil briskly without stirring, until it begins to thicken, but has not browned. This temperature should be 113°C/236°F on a sugar thermometer; or when the sugar mixture will form a small ball when dropped into a bowl of cold water

3. Beat the egg yolks in a large bowl with an electric mixer, until they are pale and thick.

4. Pour the sugar syrup quickly, in a thin steady stream, into the whisked egg yolks, beating constantly with the electric beater.

5. Continue beating in this way until the mixture is thick, smooth and creamy. Allow to cool at room temperature.

6. Still using the electric mixer, beat the softened butter a spoonful at a time, into the egg and sugar mixture. Whisk well to ensure that it is evenly distributed. Chill the mixture until it reaches spreading consistency.

7. Line a 20cm/8-inch square tin with greased foil or silicone paper.

8. Cut the sponge fingers into neat pieces to enable you to use them to line the cake tin.

9. Divide the butter cream in half and spread a little of the butter cream lightly on one side of each biscuit and place them, icing side down, into the tin.

10. Cut any small pieces of biscuits to fill any corners, if necessary.

11. Continue spreading the butter cream on the biscuits and lining the cake tin in this way, alternating the direction of the fingers between the layers.

12. Sprinkle half of the brandy over the sponge biscuits, then continue spreading the remainder of the sponge with just half of the butter cream and filling the cake tin completely. Sprinkle with the remaining brandy, then chill in the refrigerator overnight.

13. Remove the cake from the tin and peel off the paper or foil. Slide the cake onto a flat surface and coat with the remaining half of the butter cream.

14. Press the chopped almonds on to the sides of the cake and decorate the top with the grated chocolate. Serve immediately, or chill in the refrigerator until required.

Cook's Notes

Time
Preparation takes about 45 minutes, plus overnight chilling.

Freezing
This cake freezes well.

Variation
The icing may be flavoured with 10ml/2 tsps instant coffee powder, which should be added when making the syrup.

Vitamin Content
Butter contains vitamins A, B and D, and eggs contain vitamins B and E. Nuts contain vitamins B and E.

LOW
CALORIE

Introduction

Keeping a check on your weight is probably one of the best ways to improve your general health. By eating a nutritionally balanced, calorie-controlled diet you will be helping your body to become fitter and to function more efficiently. Being overweight increases the chances of high blood pressure, thrombosis and heart attack, it makes keeping fit more difficult and often leaves people with low self-esteem. This is not to suggest that we should all be 'model-girl slim'. Watching your weight simply means sustaining a healthy weight for your height and age.

Whether you are on a weight-reducing diet or are simply trying to sustain your present weight, it is important to balance the food you consume against the benefits obtained from it. A chocolate milkshake will provide you with a few important nutrients, but it will not provide you with sufficient amounts of fibre, vitamins or protein for one meal, nor will it educate you to rely upon a well balanced and regular diet.

Calorie counting is in fact an ideal way of checking, on a daily basis, that you are consuming the correct amount of calories to stay at your present weight. If the amount of calories being consumed does not exceed the amount of calories being expended, a constant body weight will be maintained. In this respect the significance of regular exercise cannot be ignored – the more active you are the easier weight control becomes. There are no fast solutions to maintaining a healthy weight, a nutritionally balanced, calorie-controlled diet in conjunction with regular exercise is the healthiest and most natural answer.

These recipes have been compiled to help you plan a regular pattern of eating which is both low in calories and high in enjoyment. All the recipes are calorie counted so all you have to do is set a realistic daily allowance and decide which of the easily prepared meals to include in your menu.

SERVES 4
44 kilocalories per serving

CARROT SOUP

Carrots make a most delicious soup which is both filling and extremely low in calories.

450g/1lb carrots
1 medium-sized onion
1 medium-sized turnip
2 cloves garlic, crushed
750ml/1¼ pints water or vegetable stock
2.5ml/½ tsp dried thyme
2.5ml/½ tsp ground nutmeg
Salt and ground white pepper, to taste
Toasted sunflower seeds, flaked almonds and pistachio nuts, mixed together for garnish

1. Peel the carrots and cut them into thick slices.

2. Peel and roughly chop the onion and turnip.

3. Put the vegetables, garlic and water or stock, into a large saucepan and bring to the boil. Cover the pan, reduce the heat and simmer for 20 minutes.

4. Add all the seasonings and simmer for a further 5 minutes.

5. Remove the soup from the heat and allow to cool for 15 minutes.

6. Using a liquidiser or food processor, blend the soup until it is thick and smooth.

7. Reheat the soup as required, garnishing with the seeds and nuts before serving.

Step 2 Using a sharp knife, roughly chop the peeled onions and turnip.

Step 1 Cut the carrots into thick slices, approximately 1.25cm/½-inch thick.

Step 6 Purée the soup in a liquidiser or food processor, until it is thick and smooth.

Cook's Notes

Time
Preparation takes about 12 minutes, cooking takes 25-30 minutes.

Cook's Tip
Make the recipe in double quantities and freeze half for a future date.

Variation
Use 1.25ml/¼ tsp cayenne pepper in place of the nutmeg in this recipe.

SERVES 4
115 kilocalories per serving

MELON AND PROSCIUTTO

This typically Italian starter is wonderful served well chilled on warm summer days.

1 large ripe melon, either Galia or Honeydew
16 thin slices prosciutto ham
French flat leaf parsley to garnish

Step 1 Using a spoon, scoop out and discard the seeds and fibrous core of the melon.

Step 2 Carefully remove the rind from the quartered melon, using a sharp knife.

Step 4 Roll a slice of prosciutto ham around each thin slice of melon.

1. Cut the melon in half lengthways. Using a spoon, scoop out and discard all the seeds and fibres.

2. Cut the melon into quarters and carefully peel away the skin using a sharp knife.

3. Cut each quarter into 4 thin slices.

4. Wrap each slice of melon in a slice of the prosciutto ham, and arrange on a serving dish. Chill well and garnish with parsley before serving.

Cook's Notes

Time
Preparation takes 15 minutes.

Cook's Tip
Use this recipe, along with other items such as olives, stuffed eggs and sliced salami, as Italian antipasta for a buffet party.

Variation
Serve the slices of prosciutto ham in rolls, accompanied by quartered fresh figs in place of the melon.

SERVES 4

24 kilocalories per serving

ORANGE, GRAPEFRUIT AND MINT SALAD

*Fresh citrus fruits are complemented beautifully by the fragrant flavour of
fresh mint. Serve chilled for an ideal
low calorie starter.*

2 grapefruits
3 oranges
Liquid sweetener to taste (optional)
8 sprigs of mint

1. Using a serrated knife, cut away the peel and the white pith from the grapefruit and the oranges.

2. Carefully cut inside the skin of each segment to remove each section of flesh.

3. Squeeze the membranes over a bowl to extract all the juice. Sweeten the juice with the liquid sweetener, if required.

4. Arrange the orange and the grapefruit segments in alternating colours on 4 individual serving dishes.

5. Using a sharp knife, chop 4 springs of the mint very finely. Stir the chopped mint into the fruit juice.

6. Carefully spoon the juice over the arranged fruit segments and chill thoroughly.

7. Garnish with a sprig of mint before serving.

Step 1 Using a serrated knife, cut away the peel from the grapefruits and the oranges, making sure that you remove all the white pith as you cut.

Step 2 Carefully cut inside the skin of each segment to remove each section of flesh, trying to keep each piece as intact as possible.

Cook's Notes

Time
Preparation takes about 20 minutes, plus chilling time.

Cook's Tip
This starter can be prepared up to a day in advance.

Preparation
Make sure all the white pith is removed from the fruit, as it produces a bitter flavour.

Variation
Use ruby grapefruits and blood oranges, when available, in place of the normal types of fruit for a colourful variation. Use borage leaves in place of the mint, and garnish with a few of the blue flowers.

SERVES 4
41 kilocalories per serving

INDIAN TOMATO SOUP

This highly fragrant and spicy tomato soup makes an interesting low calorie starter.

225g/8oz tomatoes
1 medium-sized onion
30ml/2 tbsps vegetable oil
1 green chilli, seeded and finely chopped
3 cloves garlic, crushed
15ml/1 tbsp tomato purée
1 ltr/1¾ pints water, or vegetable stock
4-6 green curry leaves, or 2.5ml/½ tsp curry powder
Freshly ground sea salt, to taste
Coriander leaves and green chillies for garnish

1. Cut a small cross in the skin of each tomato and plunge them into boiling water for 30-40 seconds.

2. Remove the tomatoes and carefully peel away the loosened skin with a sharp knife.

3. Remove the green core from the tomatoes and roughly chop the flesh.

4. Peel the onion and chop it into small pieces using a sharp knife.

5. Heat the oil in a large saucepan and gently sauté the onion, chopped chilli and garlic for 3-4 minutes until it is soft, but not browned.

6. Stir in the chopped tomatoes and cook for 5 minutes, stirring often to prevent the vegetables from burning.

7. Blend the tomato purée with the water and pour this into the onions and tomatoes. Add the curry leaves or powder, season with the salt and simmer for 5-7 minutes.

8. Remove the soup from the heat and stir in the coriander leaves and the chilli halves.

9. Pour the soup into 4-6 serving bowls and serve piping hot, discarding the chilli garnish before eating.

Step 2 Remove the tomatoes from the boiling water and carefully peel away the loosened skin.

Step 3 Cut away and discard the hard green core from the tomatoes, and chop the flesh roughly with a sharp knife.

Cook's Notes

Time
Preparation takes about 15 minutes, cooking takes 17-18 minutes.

Watchpoint
Great care must be taken when preparing fresh chillies. Try not to get the juice into your eyes or mouth. If this should happen, rinse with lots of cold water.

Freezing
This soup freezes well, but should be frozen before adding the garnish.

SERVES 2
252 kilocalories per serving

FRESH TOMATO OMELETTE

Omelettes can make substantial low calorie lunches or light meals and can be varied by using different fillings. This recipe uses lots of tasty fresh tomatoes, which can be eaten in abundance on a calorie controlled diet.

450g/1lb fresh tomatoes
Salt and freshly ground black pepper
4 eggs
60ml/4 tbsps water
2.5ml/½ tsp fresh chopped basil
30ml/2 tbsps olive or vegetable oil
2.5ml/½ tsp fresh chopped oregano or basil to garnish

1. Cut a small cross into the skins of each tomato and plunge them into boiling water. Leave for 30 seconds, then remove them with a draining spoon.

2. Using a sharp knife carefully peel away the tomato skins and discard them.

3. Cut the tomatoes in half and remove and discard the seeds, juice and any tough core.

4. Cut the tomato flesh into thin strips.

5. Break the eggs into a bowl and whisk in the water and chopped herbs. Season with salt and pepper and continue whisking until the egg mixture is frothy.

6. Heat the oil in a large frying pan or skillet, then pour in the egg mixture.

7. Using a spatula, stir the egg mixture around the skillet for about 2-3 minutes, or until the eggs are beginning to set.

8. Spread the tomato strips over the partially cooked eggs, and continue cooking without stirring until the eggs have completely set and the tomatoes are just warmed through.

9. Sprinkle with the additional chopped basil before serving.

Step 2 Carefully peel away and discard the tomato skins from the blanched fruit, using a sharp knife.

Step 3 Remove the seeds and juice from the halved tomatoes with a teaspoon.

Step 5 Whisk the eggs, water and herbs together thoroughly, until they are frothy.

Cook's Notes

Time
Preparation takes about 25 minutes, cooking takes about 5 minutes.

Variation
Add 1 clove of crushed garlic to the egg mixture, if desired.

Serving Idea
Cut the omelette into wedges and serve straight from the frying pan.

SERVES 4

83 kilocalories per serving

VEGETABLE KEBABS

*A colourful and flavoursome way to serve delicious fresh vegetables as part of
a low calorie diet.*

1 large aubergine
Salt
1 large green pepper
4 courgettes
12-14 cherry tomatoes, red or yellow
12-14 pickling onions
12-14 button mushrooms
60ml/4 tbsps olive oil
30ml/2 tbsps lemon juice
2.5ml/½ tsp salt
2.5ml/½ tsp freshly ground black pepper

1. Cut the aubergine in half and dice it into 2.5cm/1-inch pieces.

2. Put the aubergine pieces into a large bowl, and sprinkle liberally with salt. Stir well and allow to stand for 30 minutes to degorge.

3. Rinse the aubergine pieces thoroughly in a colander under cold water, to remove all traces of salt.

4. Cut the green pepper in half. Remove and discard the core and seeds. Cut the pepper flesh into 2.5cm/1-inch pieces with a sharp knife.

5. Slice the courgette diagonally into pieces approximately 2.5cm/1-inch thick.

6. Remove the tough cores form the cherry tomatoes and peel the onions. Rinse the mushrooms under cold water to remove any bits of soil, but do not peel.

7. Put all the prepared vegetables into a large bowl and pour in the remaining ingredients. Mix well to coat evenly, cover with plastic wrap and allow to stand for about 30 minutes, stirring the vegetables once or twice to ensure they remain evenly coated.

8. Thread the vegetables alternately onto skewers and arrange them on a grill pan.

9. Brush the kebabs with the marinade and grill for 3-4 minutes, turning frequently and basting with the marinade until they are evenly browned. Serve piping hot.

Step 5 Cut the courgettes diagonally into 2.5cm/1-inch pieces.

Step 8 Thread the prepared and marinated vegetables alternately onto kebab skewers, keeping an even number of vegetable pieces on each skewer.

Cook's Notes

Time
Preparation takes about 30 minutes. Cooking takes about 10 minutes, plus time for the vegetables to marinate.

Preparation
It is important to degorge the aubergines before cooking, as this removes the bitterness from the flavour and some of the moisture as well.

Variation
Use any combination of your favourite vegetables in this recipe.

SERVES 6
213 kilocalories per serving

DOLMAS

Delicious individual parcels of rice, herbs, nuts and fruit, make a very different low calorie lunch or supper dish.

12 large cabbage leaves, washed
180g/6oz long grain rice
8 spring onions
15ml/1 tbsp fresh chopped basil
15ml/1 tbsp fresh chopped mint
15ml/1 tbsp fresh chopped parsley
60g/2oz pine nuts
60g/2oz currants
Salt and freshly ground black pepper
60ml/4 tbsps olive oil
Juice 1 lemon
140ml/¼ pint unset natural yogurt
120g/4oz cucumber

Step 5 Pile tablespoons of the filling onto the blanched leaves, pressing it gently into sausage shapes in the centre of the leaves.

1. Using a sharp knife trim away any tough stems from the cabbage leaves.

2. Put the leaves into boiling water for about 30 seconds. Remove them using a slotted spoon and drain thoroughly before laying them out flat on a work surface.

3. Put the rice into a saucepan along with enough boiling water to just cover. Cook for 15-20 minutes, or until the rice is soft and the liquid almost completely absorbed. Rinse the rice in cold water to remove any starchiness.

4. Cut the spring onions into thin diagonal slices. Put the rice and the chopped onions into a large bowl along with all the remaining ingredients, except 30ml/2 tbsps olive oil, the yogurt and cucumber. Mix the rice mixture thoroughly to blend evenly.

5. Place about 30ml/2 tbsps of the rice filling onto each blanched cabbage leaf, pressing it gently into a sausage shape.

6. Fold the sides of the leaves over to partially cover the stuffing, and then roll up, Swiss roll fashion, to completely envelop the filling.

7. Place the rolls seam side down in a large baking dish. Brush with the remaining olive oil. Pour hot water around the cabbage leaves until it comes about halfway up their sides.

8. Cover the baking dish with aluminium foil, pressing it gently onto the surface of the leaves to keep them in place. Bake in a preheated oven 190°C/375°F/Gas Mark 5 for 30-40 minutes.

9. Peel the cucumber and cut it lengthways into quarters. Remove the pips and discard. Chop the cucumber flesh and half of the peel into very small pieces.

10. Mix the chopped cucumber into the yogurt and chill until required.

11. Drain the dolmas from the cooking liquid and arrange on a serving plate with a little of the cucumber sauce spooned over.

Cook's Notes

Time
Preparation takes about 30 minutes, cooking takes 40 minutes.

Serving Idea
Serve the dolmas either hot or cold.

Preparation
Dolmas can be prepared a day in advance and allowed to stand in their liquid in the refrigerator. They can be reheated just before serving if required.

Variation
Use any other ingredients you particularly like in the filling along with the rice. Use vine leaves instead of cabbage leaves in this recipe.

SERVES 6
156 kilocalories per serving

AUBERGINE BAKE

Aubergines are wonderfully filling vegetables with very few calories – the ideal ingredient in a calorie controlled diet.

2 large or 3 medium-sized aubergines
10ml/2 tsps salt
140ml/¼ pint malt vinegar
30ml/2 tbsps vegetable oil
2 large onions, peeled and sliced into rings
2 green chillies, seeded and finely chopped
425g/15oz can peeled plum tomatoes, chopped
2.5ml/½ tsp chilli powder
5ml/1 tsp crushed garlic
2.5ml/½ tsp ground turmeric
8 tomatoes, sliced
280ml/½ pint natural unset yogurt
5ml/1 tsp freshly ground black pepper
90g/3oz Cheddar cheese, finely grated

1. Cut the aubergines into 5mm/¼-inch thick slices. Arrange the slices in a shallow dish and sprinkle with 5ml/1 tsp of the salt. Pour over the malt vinegar, cover the dish and marinate for 30 minutes.

2. Drain the aubergine well, discarding the marinade liquid.

3. Heat the vegetable oil in a frying pan and gently fry the onion rings until they are golden brown.

4. Add the chillies, the remaining salt, chopped tomatoes, chilli powder, garlic and turmeric. Mix well and simmer for 5-7 minutes until thick and well blended.

5. Remove the sauce from the heat and cool slightly. Blend to a smooth purée using a liquidiser or food processor.

6. Arrange half of the aubergine slices in the base of a lightly greased shallow ovenproof dish.

7. Spoon half of the tomato sauce over the aubergine slices. Cover the tomato sauce with the remaining aubergine, and then top this with the remaining tomato sauce and sliced tomatoes.

8. Mix together the yogurt, the freshly ground black pepper and the Cheddar cheese. Pour this mixture over the tomato slices.

9. Preheat an oven to 190°C/375°F/Gas Mark 5, and cook the aubergine bake for 20-30 minutes, or until the cheese topping bubbles and turns golden brown. Serve hot straight from the oven.

Step 4 Fry the chillies, tomatoes and seasoning with the golden onion rings until they are softened and juice flows.

Step 7 Spoon half the tomato sauce over the aubergine slices in the gratin dish.

Cook's Notes

Time
Preparation takes about 30 minutes, cooking takes 40 minutes.

Preparation
Make sure that the aubergines are well drained when they are removed from the marinade. Press them into a colander using the back of your hand, to remove all excess vinegar. Do not rinse, as the vinegar gives a tangy flavour to the dish.

Cook's Tip
Use a low calorie cheese in place of the Cheddar cheese to reduce the calorie content further.

SERVES 4
54 kilocalories per serving

OKRA CASSEROLE

Okra has an interesting texture and a mild flavour which combines well with tomatoes to make this delicious Mediterranean-style casserole.

30ml/2 tbsps olive oil
1 small onion
225g/8oz fresh okra
6 ripe tomatoes
Juice of ½ lemon
Salt and freshly ground black pepper
30ml/2 tbsps fresh chopped parsley

1. Peel the onions and cut them in half lengthways. Use a sharp knife to cut them across in slices.

2. Heat the oil in a large saucepan and cook the onion until it is soft and transparent, but not browned.

3. Remove just the stems from the okra, but leave on the pointed tail. Take care not to cut off the very top of the okra.

4. Add the okra to the onions and cook gently for 10 minutes, stirring occasionally.

5. Cut a small cross into the skins of the tomatoes, and plunge them into boiling water for 30 seconds.

6. Drain the tomatoes and carefully peel away and discard the loosened skins. Chop the peeled fruit roughly.

7. Add the tomatoes, lemon juice, seasoning and parsley to the okra, and continue to cook for about 5 more minutes, or until the tomatoes are just heated through.

8. Spoon into a serving dish and serve hot or cold.

Step 3 Trim just the stems from the top of the okra, but take care not to remove the whole top, or the pointed tails.

Step 1 Place the halved peeled onions cut side downwards, and use a sharp knife to cut across into thin slices.

Step 6 Carefully peel the skins away from the blanched tomatoes, using a sharp knife.

Cook's Notes

Time
Preparation takes 15 minutes, cooking takes approximately 15 minutes.

Variation
Green beans can be used in place of the okra.

Cook's Tip
If you cannot get fresh okra, use canned okra in its place, but drain and rinse this before use and cut the cooking time in half.

Watchpoint
If too much liquid is left at the end of cooking, remove the vegetables with a slotted spoon and boil the liquid quickly to reduce the sauce.

SERVES 6
234 kilocalories per serving

PASTA WITH FRESH TOMATO AND BASIL SAUCE

Pasta is a good item to include on a low calorie diet, as it is very filling and can be served with any variety of low calorie sauces.

1 small onion, finely chopped
450g/1lb fresh tomatoes
30ml/2 tbsps tomato purée
1 orange
2 cloves garlic, crushed
Salt and freshly ground black pepper
140ml/¼ pint red wine
140ml/¼ pint chicken stock
30ml/2 tbsps coarsely chopped basil
340g/12oz wholemeal pasta

1. Peel and finely chop the onion.

2. Cut a small cross in the skins of the tomatoes and plunge them into boiling water for 30 seconds. Remove the blanched tomatoes from the water and carefully peel away the loosened skin.

3. Cut the tomatoes into quarters, and remove and discard the pips. Chop the tomato flesh roughly, and put this, the onion and the tomato purée into a large saucepan.

4. Heat the onion and tomatoes over a gentle heat, stirring continuously until the tomatoes soften and begin to lose their juice.

5. Finely grate the rind from the orange. Cut the orange in half and squeeze out the juice.

6. Put the orange, rind and juice into a large saucepan along with all the remaining ingredients, and bring to the boil.

Step 1 To chop an onion finely, pierce the peeled onion with a fork and use this to hold the vegetable steady whilst you chop with a sharp knife.

Step 3 Cut the tomatoes into quarters and remove and discard the seeds.

7. Continue to boil until the sauce has reduced and thickened and the vegetables are soft.

8. Whilst the sauce is cooking, put the pasta into another saucepan with enough boiling water to cover. Season with a little salt and cook for 10-15 minutes, or until the pasta is soft.

9. Drain the pasta in a colander, and stir it into the hot sauce. Serve at once with a salad.

Cook's Notes

Time
Preparation takes 15-20 minutes, cooking takes 10-15 minutes.

Variation
Add 120g/4oz thinly sliced mushrooms to the sauce, if liked.

Freezing
This sauce will freeze very well for up to 3 months.

SERVES 6
153 kilocalories per serving

VEGETABLE AND OLIVE CASSEROLE

The addition of vinegar and capers gives this refreshing vegetable dish a sharp twist to its flavour.

1 aubergine
Salt
140ml/¼ pint olive, or vegetable oil
1 onion, peeled and thinly sliced
2 red peppers, seeded and chopped
2 sticks of celery, sliced thickly
450g/1lb canned plum tomatoes
30ml/2 tbsps red wine vinegar
15ml/1 tbsp sugar
1 clove garlic, crushed
12 black olives, pitted
15ml/1 tbsp capers
Salt and freshly ground black pepper

1. Cut the aubergine in half lengthways and score the cut surface deeply, in a lattice fashion, with the point of a sharp knife.

2. Sprinkle the cut surface of the aubergine liberally with salt, and leave to stand for 30 minutes.

3. Rinse the aubergines thoroughly under running water, then pat dry and cut it into 2.5cm/1-inch cubes.

4. Heat the oil in a large sauté pan and add the onion, peppers and celery. Cook gently for about 5 minutes, stirring occasionally until the vegetables have softened but not browned.

5. Add the aubergine to the pan and mix well to coat thoroughly with the oil. Continue cooking gently for 5 minutes.

6. Chop the plum tomatoes and then press them through a nylon sieve, using the back of a wooden spoon to press out all the juice and pulp, leaving the seeds and pith in the sieve.

7. Add the sieved tomatoes to the vegetables in the sauté pan, along with the remaining ingredients, except for the olives and capers. Cover and simmer for 5 minutes.

8. Cut the olives into quarters and add these to the simmering vegetables, along with the capers.

9. Continue cooking gently, uncovered, for a further 15 minutes, or until most of the liquid has evaporated and the sauce has thickened and reduced.

Step 1 Score the cut surface of the aubergines in a lattice pattern, using the point of a sharp knife.

Step 9 Simmer the casserole, uncovered, over a low heat until the juice has thickened and reduced.

Cook's Notes

Time
Preparation takes 30 minutes, plus 30 minutes for the aubergines to degorge. Cooking takes approximately 25 minutes.

Preparation
Scoring and salting the aubergine will remove any bitter taste and toughness from the vegetable. Be very sure, however, to rinse all the salt off the aubergines before cooking, or this will affect the flavour of the dish.

Cook's Tip
This recipe may be prepared 2-3 days in advance and kept covered in a refrigerator.

Serving Idea
This recipe is delicious served cold as a salad, or hot with rice and pitta bread.

SERVES 6
21 kilocalories per serving

SALADE PAYSANNE

This homely salad can be made with any selection of fresh vegetables you have to hand. So whether its winter or summer, there's no excuse for not serving a delicious fresh salad.

4 spring onions
½ cucumber
3 carrots
6 large tomatoes
10 button mushrooms
3 stems celery
1 green pepper, seeded and chopped
15-20 tiny cauliflower florets
15-20 radishes, quartered
15ml/1 tbsp chopped watercress, or mustard and cress
2 sprigs fresh green coriander leaf, or chopped parsley
2.5ml/½ tsp salt
2.5ml/½ tsp freshly ground black pepper
30ml/2 tbsps cider vinegar
15ml/1 tbsp lemon juice
60ml/4 tbsps olive or vegetable oil
Pinch mustard powder
Liquid sweetener to taste
8 lettuce leaves for garnish

1. Trim the spring onions and slice them diagonally into thin slices.

2. Peel the cucumber and quarter it lengthways. Use a sharp knife to remove the soft, seedy centre, discard this, and dice the remaining flesh.

3. Peel and carrots and slice them thinly, cutting the carrots diagonally with a sharp knife.

4. Cut a small cross into the skins of each tomato, and plunge into boiling water for 30 seconds. Remove the tomatoes and carefully peel away the blanched skin from the fruit. Quarter the peeled tomatoes and cut away the tough green stalk.

5. Thinly slice the mushrooms and sticks of celery.

6. Cut the pepper in half lengthways and remove all the seeds and the white pith. Discard this, and chop the flesh.

Step 3 Cut the carrot into thin pieces, slicing diagonally with a sharp knife.

Step 9 Whisk all the dressing ingredients together using a fork or balloon whisk, until the mixture becomes thick and cloudy.

7. Break the cauliflower florets into small pieces, and quarter the radishes.

8. Roughly chop the watercress, or mustard and cress, along with the coriander leaves or parsley.

9. For the dressing mix together all the remaining ingredients, except for the lettuce leaves. Whisk thoroughly using a fork, or balloon whisk, until the mixture becomes thick and cloudy.

10. Arrange the lettuce leaves on a serving dish, and pile the prepared vegetables on top.

11. Just before serving, spoon a little of the dressing over the salad and serve the remainder separately in a small jug.

Cook's Notes

Time
Preparation takes about 20 minutes.

Variation
Use any combination of your own favourite vegetables in this recipe.

Serving Idea
Serve with cheese or chicken for a light lunch.

SERVES 4
87 kilocalories per serving

BLACK OLIVE AND CAULIFLOWER SALAD

The exciting flavours of the Mediterranean combine in this recipe to produce a refreshingly different salad.

120g/4oz black olives
1 large cauliflower
1 large Spanish onion
60ml/4 tbsps olive oil
140ml/¼ pint water
Juice ½ lemon
45ml/3 tbsps tomato purée
Salt and freshly ground black pepper
30ml/2 tbsps fresh chopped parsley

Step 1 To loosen the stones before pitting, roll the olives firmly on a flat surface using the palm of your hand.

1. Roll the olives firmly on a flat surface with the palm of your hands to loosen the stones. Remove the stones using a cherry pitter or the tip of a potato peeler. Chop the olives roughly and set aside.

2. Trim the leaves from the cauliflower and break it into small florets.

3. Peel the onion and slice it into rings.

4. Heat the oil in a large sauté pan and gently cook the cauliflower for 2 minutes. Remove the cauliflower to a plate, and cook the onion in the same pan, in the same way.

5. Return the cauliflower to the pan and add the water and the lemon juice. Bring to the boil, reduce the heat and simmer until tender, adding a little more water should the mixture begin to boil dry.

6. Using a slotted spoon, remove the cauliflower from the sauté pan, reserving the juices.

Step 3 Slice the onion into rings by piercing the peeled vegetable with a fork to hold it steady whilst you slice.

7. Add the tomato purée to the liquid and boil rapidly to reduce.

8. Stir the olives into the pan and heat through.

9. Arrange the cauliflower florets on a serving dish, and spoon the olive sauce over the top. Chill well.

10. Sprinkle with the chopped parsley just before serving.

Cook's Notes

Time
Preparation takes about 20 minutes, cooking takes approximately 20 minutes, plus chilling time.

Cook's Tip
Add a bay leaf to the cauliflower during the cooking to reduce the strong smell.

Variation
Use green olives instead of black.

SERVES 4

99 kilocalories per serving

STIR-FRIED SALAD

Stir fries are served hot, but the ingredients are cooked so quickly that they retain all of their crunchiness.

1 onion
2 large leeks
60ml/4 tbsps olive oil
2 cloves garlic, crushed
225g/8oz mange tout peas, topped and tailed
120g/4oz bean sprouts, or lentil sprouts
Salt and freshly ground black pepper
15ml/1 tbsp fresh chopped coriander leaf

1. Peel the onion and cut it into thin rings.

Step 1 Pierce the onion with a fork to hold it steady whilst you slice it into thin rings.

2. Trim the leeks and cut down the length of one side. Open the leek out and wash it thoroughly under running water.

3. Cut the leek into three pieces, then thinly slice each piece lengthways into thin strips.

4. Heat the oil in a large wok or frying pan, and add the onions and garlic. Cook for 2 minutes, stirring all the time until the onions have softened but not browned.

5. Add the mange tout and sliced leeks to the wok and continue stir-frying for 4 minutes.

6. Add the remaining ingredients and cook briskly for a further 2 minutes. Serve piping hot.

Step 2 Rinse the split leek under running water, separating the leaves to wash out any grit or dirt.

Step 3 Cut the pieces of leek lengthways into thin strips.

Cook's Notes

Time
Preparation takes 15 minutes, cooking takes approximately 10 minutes.

Cook's Tip
Sprout your own beans or lentils by putting them into a glass jar, rinse thoroughly and pour in fresh water each day, cover with muslin, and stand the jar on a sunny windowsill. After 3-4 days, the beans or lentils will have sprouted.

Serving Idea
Serve this dish with rice, and sprinkle it liberally with soy sauce.

SERVES 6
84 kilocalories per serving

RATATOUILLE

This delicious vegetable casserole from the south of France has become a great favourite the world over.

2 aubergines
Salt
4 courgettes
60ml/4 tbsps olive oil
2 Spanish onions
2 green or red peppers
10ml/2 tsps chopped fresh basil
1 large clove garlic, crushed
2 x 793g/1lb 12 oz cans of peeled plum tomatoes
Salt and freshly ground black pepper
140ml/¼ pint dry white wine

1. Cut the aubergines in half lengthways and score each cut surface diagonally, using the point of a sharp knife.

2. Sprinkle the aubergines liberally with salt and allow to stand for 30 minutes to degorge. After this time, rinse them thoroughly and pat them dry.

3. Roughly chop the aubergines and slice the courgettes thickly. Set them to one side.

4. Peel the onions and half them. Cut them into thin slices with a sharp knife.

5. Cut the peppers in half lengthways and remove and discard the seeds and white pith. Chop the flesh roughly.

6. Heat the oil in a large saucepan, and fry the onion slices for 5 minutes until they are soft and just beginning to brown.

7. Stir in the peppers and courgettes, and cook gently for 5 minutes until they begin to soften. Remove all the vegetables from the pan and set them aside.

8. Put the chopped aubergines into the saucepan with

Step 5 Remove and discard the seeds and white pith from the halved peppers.

Step 8 Gently fry the chopped aubergine in the vegetable juices and oil, until they begin to brown.

the vegetable juices. Cook gently until it begins to brown, then add all the other ingredients to the pan.

9. Add the cans of tomatoes, the garlic and the basil to the saucepan along with the sautéed vegetables, mixing well to blend in evenly. Bring to the boil, then reduce the heat and simmer for 15 minutes, or until the liquid in the pan has been reduced and is thick.

10. Add the wine to the pan and continue cooking for a further 15 minutes, before serving straight away, or chilling and serving cold.

Cook's Notes

Time
Preparation takes 20 minutes, plus 30 minutes standing time. Cooking takes approximately 35 minutes.

Preparation
Make sure that the degorged aubergine is rinsed thoroughly to remove any saltiness, otherwise this will spoil the flavour of the finished dish.

Cook's Tip
If the liquid in the pan is still thin and excessive after the full cooking time, remove the vegetables and boil the juices rapidly until they have reduced and thickened.

SERVES 4
239 kilocalories per serving

LIME ROASTED CHICKEN

This simply made, but unusual, main course is very low in calories and high in tangy flavour.

---

4 chicken breast portions, each weighing about
   225g/8oz
Salt and freshly ground black pepper
4 limes
10ml/2 tsps white wine vinegar
75ml/5 tbsps olive oil
10ml/2 tsp fresh chopped basil

---

1. Rub the chicken portions all over with salt and black pepper. Place in a shallow ovenproof dish, and set aside.

2. Carefully pare away thin strips of the rind only from 2 of the limes, using a lemon parer. Cut these 2 limes in half and squeeze the juice.

3. Add the lime juice to the vinegar and 4 tbsps of the olive oil in a small dish, along with the strips of rind, and mix well.

4. Pour the oil and lime juice mixture over the chicken por-tions in the dish. Cover and refrigerate for about 4 hours or overnight.

5. Remove the covering from the dish in which the chicken is marinating, and baste the chicken well with the marinade mixture. Place into a preheated oven 190°C/375°F/ Gas Mark 5 and cook for 30-35 minutes, or until the chicken is well roasted and tender.

6. In the meantime, peel away the rind and white pith from the remaining 2 limes. Cut the limes into thin slices using a sharp knife.

7. Heat the remaining oil in a small frying pan and add the lime slices and basil. Cook quickly for 1 minute, or until the fragrance rises up from the basil and the limes just begin to soften.

8. Serve the chicken portions on a serving platter, garnished with the fried lime slices and a little extra fresh basil, if desired.

Step 5 After marinating for 4 hours, the chicken portions will look slightly cooked and the meat will have turned a pale opaque colour.

Step 7 Fry the lime slices very quickly in the hot oil until they just begin to soften.

Cook's Notes

Time
Preparation takes 25 minutes, plus 4 hours marinating time. Cooking takes 40 minutes.

Preparation
The chicken can be prepared in advance and marinated overnight.

Variation
Use lemons instead of limes, and thyme instead of basil.

Watchpoint
Puncture the chicken with a skewer at its thickest point and when the resulting juices run clear, it is ready.

SERVES 4

300 kilocalories per serving

CHICKEN ESCALOPES

Chicken is an excellent meat to eat when on a low calorie diet, as it is extremely low in fat. There are a multitude of different methods of cooking chicken, and this one although one of the simplest, is also one of the most delicious.

4 chicken breasts, boned and skinned
1 egg white
120ml/8 tbsps wholemeal breadcrumbs
15ml/1 tbsp chopped fresh sage
Salt and freshly ground black pepper
30ml/2 tbsps walnut oil
120ml/4 fl oz low calorie mayonnaise
140ml/¼ pint natural unset yogurt
5ml/1 tsp grated fresh horseradish
30ml/2 tbsps chopped walnuts
Lemon slices and chopped walnuts to garnish

1. Pat the chicken breasts dry with kitchen paper.

2. Whisk the egg whites with a fork until they just begin to froth, but are still liquid.

3. Carefully brush all surfaces of the chicken breasts with the beaten egg white.

4. Put the breadcrumbs onto a shallow plate and mix in the chopped sage. Season with a little salt and freshly ground black pepper.

5. Place the chicken breasts, one at a time, onto the plate of breadcrumbs and sage, and carefully press this mixture onto the surfaces of the chicken.

6. Put the oil into a large shallow pan, and gently fry the prepared chicken breasts on each side for 5 minutes until they are lightly golden and tender. Set them aside, and keep warm.

7. Mix all the remaining ingredients except for the garnish, in a small bowl, whisking well to blend the yogurt and mayonnaise evenly.

8. Place the cooked chicken breasts on a serving dish, and spoon a little of the sauce over. Serve garnished with the lemon slices and additional chopped nuts.

Step 2 Whisk the egg white with a fork until it becomes frothy, but still liquid.

Step 5 Press the breadcrumb and sage mixture onto all surfaces of the chicken breasts, making sure that they are covered evenly.

Cook's Notes

Time
Preparation takes about 20 minutes, cooking takes 10-15 minutes.

Variation
Use almonds instead of walnuts in this recipe, and limes instead of lemons. Oranges and hazelnuts make another delicious variation.

Serving Idea
Serve with lightly cooked French beans and new potatoes, or rice.

SERVES 4
230 kilocalories per serving

PAPRIKA SCHNITZEL

Thin slices of fillet pork are served with a rich tasting paprika sauce for a delicious low calorie meal.

8 thin slices fillet pork, cut along the fillet
Salt and freshly ground black pepper
1 clove garlic, crushed
45ml/3 tbsps vegetable oil
1 medium-sized onion
1 red pepper
1 green pepper
15ml/1 tbsp paprika
140ml/¼ pint beef stock
120ml/4 fl oz red wine
45ml/3 tbsps tomato purée
140ml/¼ pint natural low fat yogurt

Step 1 Flatten the pork fillets out with a rolling pin until they are 0.75 cm/¼-inch thick.

1. Trim the slices of pork to remove any fat, and flatten them out with a rolling pin until they are 0.75cm/¼-inch thick.

2. Rub both sides of the pork fillets with salt, pepper, and garlic, then allow to stand in a refrigerator for 30 minutes.

3. Heat the oil in a large frying pan, and cook the pork fillets in several batches if necessary, until they are well browned and cooked right through. This will take approximately 4 minutes on each side.

4. Remove the pork from the pan, set aside, and keep warm.

5. Peel the onion and thinly slice it into rings, steadying it with a fork as you cut. Cut the peppers in half and remove and discard the seeds and white pith. Slice the peppers lengthways into thin strips.

6. Add the onion rings and the sliced peppers to the oil and meat juices in the frying pan, and cook quickly for about 3-4 minutes until they are soft but not browned.

7. Add the paprika, stock, wine and tomato purée to the frying pan with the vegetables, and bring the mixture to the boil.

8. Reduce the heat and simmer until the liquid has evapo-

Step 6 Fry the onions and peppers together for 3-4 minutes until they have softened but not browned.

rated and the sauce has thickened. Season with salt and pepper to taste.

9. Arrange the pork slices on a serving dish, and pour the paprika sauce over the top of them.

10. Beat the yogurt in a bowl until it is smooth.

11. Carefully drizzle the yogurt over the paprika sauce to make an attractive pattern. Swirl it gently into the sauce to blend, but take care not to incorporate it completely. Serve hot.

Cook's Notes

 Time
Preparation takes 30 minutes, cooking takes approximately 20 minutes.

 Freezing
This dish freezes well.

Preparation
This dish may be made in advance, covered with foil, then re-heated in a moderate oven when required.

 Cook's Tip
If the yogurt is too thick to drizzle properly, whisk in a little water or skimmed milk to thin it to the required consistency.

SERVES 4

198 kilocalories per serving

CHICKEN WITH BLACKCURRANT SAUCE

*The sharp tang of blackcurrants makes an ideal partner
for lightly cooked chicken.*

4 chicken breasts, boned and skinned
45ml/3 tbsps sesame oil
225g/8oz fresh blackcurrants
Juice of 1 orange
140ml/¼ pint red wine
Artificial sweetener, to taste
Orange slices and fresh blackcurrants to garnish

1. Season the chicken breasts with a little salt. Heat the oil in a shallow frying pan.

Step 2 Gently fry the chicken breasts in the hot oil until they are golden brown on all sides.

2. Gently fry the chicken breasts for 4-5 minutes on each side, until they are golden brown and tender.

3. Top and tail the blackcurrants and put them into a small pan, along with the orange juice and red wine. Bring to the boil, then cover and simmer gently until the blackcurrants are soft.

4. Using a liquidiser or food processor, blend the blackcurrants and the cooking juice for 30 seconds.

Step 5 Press the blackcurrant purée through a metal sieve with a wooden spoon, to remove all the pips and skins.

Step 6 Simmer the sieved fruit purée until it has thickened and the liquid has reduced.

5. Rub the blended purée through a nylon sieve with the back of a spoon, pressing the fruit through to reserve all the juice and pulp but leaving the pips in the sieve.

6. Put the sieved purée into a small saucepan and heat gently, stirring constantly until the liquid has reduced and the sauce is thick and smooth.

7. Arrange the chicken breasts on a serving dish, and spoon the blackcurrant sauce over. Garnish with orange slices and fresh blackcurrants.

Cook's Notes

Time
Preparation takes 15 minutes, cooking takes approximately 15 minutes.

Preparation
To test if the chicken breasts are cooked, insert a skewer into the thickest part, then press gently, if the juices run clear, the meat is cooked.

Variation
Use blackberries instead of blackcurrants in this recipe.

Serving Idea
Serve with a selection of fresh green vegetables.

SERVES 4
220 kilocalories per serving

KIDNEYS WITH MUSTARD SAUCE

Lambs' kidneys have a wonderful delicate flavour, and when served with a delicious mustard sauce, make a quick and very flavoursome main course.

60ml/4 tbsps vegetable oil
675g/1½lbs lambs' kidneys
1-2 shallots, peeled and finely chopped
280ml/½ pint dry white wine
45ml/3 tbsps Dijon mustard
Salt, pepper and lemon juice, to taste
30ml/2 tbsps fresh chopped parsley

1. Cut the kidneys in half lengthways, and carefully snip out the core and tough tubes.

2. Heat the oil in a large frying pan, and gently sauté the kidneys for about 10 minutes, stirring them frequently until they are light brown on all sides. Remove the kidneys from the pan and keep them warm.

3. Add the shallots to the sauté pan and cook for about 1 minute, stirring frequently until they soften, but do not brown.

4. Add the wine and bring to the boil, stirring constantly and scraping the pan to remove any brown juices.

5. Allow the wine to boil rapidly for 3-4 minutes, until it has reduced by about 2/3rds. Remove the pan from the heat.

6. Using a balloon whisk or fork, mix the mustard into the reduced wine along with salt, pepper, lemon juice to taste, and half of the fresh chopped parsley.

7. Return the kidneys to the pan and cook over a low heat for 1-2 minutes, stirring all the time to heat the kidneys through evenly. Serve immediately, sprinkled with the remaining parsley.

Step 1 Trim any fat or tubes away from the core of each kidney, using a sharp knife or small pair of scissors.

Step 2 Sauté the kidneys in the hot oil, stirring them frequently to brown evenly on all sides.

Step 6 Using a balloon whisk or fork, blend the mustard into the reduced wine, whisking well to keep the sauce smooth.

Cook's Notes

Time
Preparation takes about 25 minutes, cooking takes 15 minutes.

Variation
Use chicken livers in place of the lambs' kidney in this recipe.

Watchpoint
Take care not to cook the kidneys for too long as they will toughen if overcooked.

SERVES 4
254 kilocalories per serving

SOLE KEBABS

*Fish is highly nutritious, economical to prepare, and makes an ideal
contribution to a healthy diet.*

---

8 fillets of sole
60ml/4 tbsps olive oil
1 clove garlic, peeled and crushed
Juice ½ lemon
Finely grated rind ½ lemon
Salt and freshly ground black pepper
3 drops of Tabasco, or pepper sauce
3 medium-sized courgettes
1 medium-sized green pepper
Freshly chopped parsley for garnish

---

1. Using a sharp knife, carefully peel the skin from the backs of each sole fillet.

Step 1 Use a sharp knife to carefully cut between the meat of the fish and the skin. Lift the meat up and away as you cut, keeping the blade of the knife away from you.

Step 2 Cut the sole fillets in half lengthways, and roll the slices up 'Swiss roll' fashion.

2. Cut each sole fillet in half lengthways, and roll each slice up 'Swiss roll' fashion.

3. Mix together the oil, garlic, lemon juice, rind, and seasonings in a small bowl.

4. Put the rolls of fish into a shallow dish and pour over the lemon and oil marinade. Cover the dish and allow to stand in a cool place for at least 2 hours.

5. Cut the courgettes into 0.5cm/¼-inch slices.

6. Cut the peppers in half lengthways and remove the white core and the seeds. Chop the pepper flesh into 2.5cm/1-inch squares.

7. Carefully thread the marinated sole fillets onto kebab skewers, alternating these with pieces of the prepared vegetables. Brush each kebab with a little of the oil and lemon marinade.

8. Arrange the kebabs on a grill pan and cook under a moderately hot grill for about 8 minutes, turning frequently to prevent them from burning, and brushing with the extra marinade to keep them moist.

9. Arrange the kebabs on a serving dish, and sprinkle with the chopped parsley for garnish.

Step 7 Thread the marinated rolls of fish onto kebab skewers, alternating these with vegetables for colour.

Cook's Notes

Time
Preparation takes about 30 minutes, plus marinating time. Cooking takes approximately 8 minutes.

Preparation
After 2 hours marinating, the sole will look opaque and have a partially cooked appearance.

Cook's Tip
These kebabs are ideal for cooking out of doors on a barbeque.

SERVES 4
157 kilocalories per serving

AUBERGINE AND CHICKEN CHILLI

This unusual dish is both delicious and filling.

2 medium-sized aubergines
60ml/4 tbsps sesame oil
2 cloves garlic, peeled and crushed
4 spring onions
1 green chilli, finely chopped
350g/12oz boned and skinned chicken breast
60ml/4 tbsps light soy sauce
30ml/2 tbsps stock, or water
15ml/1 tbsp tomato purée
5m/1 tsp cornflour
Liquid sweetener to taste

1. Cut the aubergine into quarters lengthways, using a sharp knife. Slice the aubergine quarters into pieces approximately 1.25cm/½-inch thick.

2. Put the aubergine slices into a bowl and sprinkle liberally with salt. Stir well to coat evenly. Cover with cling film and leave to stand for 30 minutes.

3. Rinse the aubergine slices very thoroughly under running water, then pat dry with a clean tea cloth.

4. Heat half of the oil in a wok, or large frying pan, and gently cook the garlic until it is soft, but not coloured.

5. Add the aubergine slices to the wok and cook, stirring frequently, for 3-4 minutes.

6. Using a sharp knife, slice the spring onions into thin

Step 6 Cut the spring onions diagonally into small pieces, approximately 1.25cm/½ inch long.

diagonal strips. Stir the spring onions together with the chilli into the cooked aubergine, and cook for a further 1 minute. Remove the aubergine and onion from the pan, and set aside, keeping warm.

7. Cut the chicken breast into thin slices with a sharp knife.

8. Heat the remaining 30ml/2 tbsps of oil in the wok, and fry the chicken pieces for approximately 2 minutes or until they have turned white and are cooked thoroughly.

9. Return the aubergine and onions to the pan and cook, stirring continuously, for 2 minutes or until heated through completely.

10. Mix together the remaining ingredients and pour these over the chicken and aubergines in the wok, stirring constantly until the sauce has thickened and cleared. Serve immediately.

Cook's Notes

Time
Preparation takes about 10 minutes, cooking takes approximately 15 minutes.

Cook's Tip
The vegetables can be prepared well in advance, but the aubergines should be removed from the salt after 30 minutes, or they will become too dehydrated.

Variation
Use turkey instead of chicken in this recipe, and courgettes in place of the aubergines.

Serving Idea
Serve this recipe as part of a more extensive Chinese style meal.

SERVES 4
170 kilocalories per serving
FRUIT PLATE

This medley of fruit can be varied to suit your taste and is served without a
syrupy liquid, so is low in calories.

1 green fig
2 kiwi fruit
2 fresh dates
1 guava
1 paw paw
120g/4oz lychees
½ small pineapple
1 fresh mango
120g/4oz seedless grapes
½ small melon
225g/8oz watermelon
30ml/2 tbsps orange juice
30ml/2 tbsps lemon juice
60g/2oz chopped walnuts, or pine kernels (optional)

1. Select a large, shallow serving platter on which to arrange the fruit.

2. Cut the figs into quarters lengthways and arrange on a plate.

3. Peel the kiwi fruits, and remove any hard core from the stem end. Slice the fruit thinly and arrange alongside the figs, reserving a few slices for the watermelon.

4. Cut the dates in half lengthways and remove the stones. Place the dates on the serving plate.

5. Cut the guavas in half and slice these into wedges with a sharp knife. Peel the paw paw and slice this into thin crescents. Arrange the guava slices and paw paw alternately onto the plate along with the other prepared fruit.

6. Peel the lychees and remove the stones from the stalk end, using the rounded tip of a swivel potato peeler. Discard the stones, and place the fruit on the serving platter.

7. Peel the pineapple and cut away any brown eyes which may remain in the flesh. Cut the pineapple into slices and remove the core, using a sharp knife or apple corer. Cut the pineapple slices into small wedges and arrange on the plate.

8. Peel the mango and cut the flesh into slices, discarding the stone.

9. Halve the seedless grapes. Place the mango and grapes in an alternate pattern, alongside the rest of the fruit on the serving plate.

10. Peel the melon, cut into half, and remove the seeds. Slice the melon flesh into small wedges.

11. Leave the peel and pips in the watermelon, and cut this into small wedges, approximately the same size as the previous melon. Arrange the melon wedges on either side of the plate and decorate with the remaining kiwi fruit if used.

12. Mix together the lemon, juice, orange juice and chopped nuts, and sprinkle this dressing evenly over the fruit on the plate. Cover with cling film and chill well before serving.

Step 6 Remove the stones from the lychees by scooping them out from the stalk end with the rounded end of a potato peeler.

Cook's Notes

Time
Preparation takes about 30 minutes, plus chilling time.

Preparation
Canned lychees could be used in place of the fresh fruit in this recipe, as could canned pineapples, kiwis and mangoes, but make sure they are packed in natural juice which should be drained before serving.

Variation
Use any selection of your favourite fruits in this recipe.

SERVES 4

63 kilocalories per serving

STRAWBERRY YOGURT ICE

Ice cream is usually forbidden on a low calorie diet, but when prepared with low fat natural yogurt and fresh fruit, it can provide a welcome treat.

225g/8oz fresh strawberries
280ml/½ pint low fat natural yogurt
10ml/2 tsps gelatin
30ml/2 tbsps boiling water
1 egg white
Liquid sweetener to taste
Few fresh strawberries for decoration

1. Remove and discard the green stalks and leaves from the top of the strawberries. Roughly chop the fruit.

2. Place the strawberries into a liquidiser, or food processor, along with the yogurt. Blend until smooth.

3. Sprinkle the gelatin over the boiling water in a small bowl. Stand the bowl into another, and pour in enough boiling water to come halfway up the sides of the dish.

4. Allow the gelatin to stand, without stirring, until it has dissolved and the liquid has cleared.

5. Pour the strawberry mixture into a bowl, and stir in the dissolved gelatin, mixing well to blend evenly. Place the bowl into a deep freeze and chill until just icy around the edges.

6. Remove the bowl from the deep freeze and beat until the chilled mixture is smooth. Return the bowl to the deep freeze and freeze once again in the same way.

7. Remove the bowl from the deep freeze a second time, and whisk with an electric mixer until smooth. Whisk the egg white until it forms soft peaks.

8. Fold the whisked egg white into the partially set straw-

Step 2 Blend the strawberries and yogurt together in a liquidiser or food processor, until they are smooth.

Step 5 Remove the strawberry mixture from the freezer when it is just beginning to set and has frozen around the edges.

berry mixture, carefully lifting and cutting the mixture to keep it light.

9. Sweeten with liquid sweetener to taste, then pour the strawberry ice into a shallow sided ice cream dish, and return to the freezer to freeze until completely set.

10. Remove the ice cream 10 minutes before serving to soften slightly. Pile into serving dishes and decorate with a few extra strawberries.

Cook's Notes

Time
Preparation takes about 15 minutes, plus freezing time.

Cook's Tip
Use frozen or canned strawberries in place of the fresh strawberries, but drain all the juice away first.

Variation
Use any other soft fruit in place of the strawberries. It may be preferable to sieve blackcurrants or raspberries to remove the pips, before adding to the yogurt as a purée.

SERVES 4

109 kilocalories per serving

BLACKBERRY FLUFF

Fresh blackberries have a delicious flavour, especially the wild ones picked from hedgerows.

1lb fresh blackberries
280ml/½ pint natural low fat set yogurt
2 egg whites
Liquid sweetener to taste
Pieces of angelica and whole blackberries to decorate

---

1. Wash the blackberries thoroughly and place them in a saucepan with no extra water, other than that which is left on their surfaces after washing. Cover the pan with a tight fitting lid, and cook over a low heat for 5-10 minutes, stirring occasionally until the fruit has softened. Cool slightly.

2. Press the cooked blackberries through a nylon sieve, using the back of a spoon to press out the juice and pulp. Discard the pips and reserve the purée.

3. Put the yogurt into a large bowl and beat in the blackberry purée until it is smooth.

4. Whisk the egg whites until they form very stiff peaks.

5. Fold these into the blackberry purée, trying not to over mix the ingredients, so as to create an attractive marbled effect.

6. Sweeten with the liquid sweetener to taste, then pile into serving dishes and decorate with the whole blackberries and angelica pieces. Chill before serving.

Step 4 Whisk the egg whites until they form very stiff peaks.

Step 5 Lightly fold the egg whites into the blackberry mixture, to create an attractive marbled effect.

Step 2 Press the cooked blackberries through a metal sieve, using the back of a wooden spoon to push through the juice and pulp, leaving the pips in the sieve.

Cook's Notes

Time
Preparation takes about 20 minutes. Cooking time takes approximately 10 minutes, plus chilling time.

Preparation
This recipe can also be partially frozen to create a cooling summer dessert.

Variation
Use raspberries, or strawberries, in place of blackberries in this recipe.

SERVES 4

101 kilocalories per serving

SUNBURST FIGS

Fresh figs can make a most attractive dessert and have the added benefit of being very low in calories.

4 fresh figs
120g/4oz redcurrants in small bunches
6 oranges
5ml/1 tsp orange flower water

1. Trim the stalks away from the top of the figs, but do not peel them.

2. Cut the figs into quarters lengthways, taking care not to sever them completely at the base.

Step 3 Carefully press open the quarters of each fig to make an attractive flower shape.

Step 2 Cut the figs into quarters lengthways with a sharp knife, taking great care not to sever the fruit completely through the base.

Step 7 Cut the orange segments away from the peeled fruit with a sharp knife, slicing carefully between the flesh and the thin membranes inside each segment.

3. Press the fig quarters open gently with your fingers, to make a flower shape. Place each fig carefully on a serving plate.

4. Arrange the small bunches of redcurrants carefully on the centre of each fig.

5. Cut 2 of the oranges in half, and squeeze out the juice. Mix this juice with the orange flower water in a small jug.

6. Carefully cut away the peel and white pith from the re-maining 4 oranges.

7. Using a sharp knife, cut the segments of orange away from the inside of the thin membranes, keeping each piece intact as a crescent shape.

8. Arrange the orange segments in between the petals of the fig flower on the serving plate.

9. Spoon equal amounts of the orange sauce over each fig, and chill thoroughly before serving.

Cook's Notes

Time
Preparation takes about 15 minutes, plus chilling time.

Variation
Use ruby grapefruit segments and blackcurrants in place of the oranges and redcurrants in this recipe.

Serving Idea
Freeze the currants before placing them on the figs, to give an attractive finish to this dessert.

SERVES 4

125 kilocalories per serving

MANGO SORBET

*This delicious cool sorbet can be used either as a dessert, or as a refresher
between courses on a low calorie meal.*

3 mangoes
Juice ½ lime
120ml/4 fl oz dry white wine
120ml/4 fl oz mineral water
1 egg white
Liquid sweetener to taste (optional)

1. Peel the mango and cut away the flesh from around the large centre stone.

2. Put the mango flesh into a liquidiser or food processor, and blend until smooth.

3. In a bowl, mix together the lime juice, wine and mineral water.

4. Place the mango purée in a freezer and freeze until just beginning to set around the edges.

5. Break up the ice crystals in the mango mixture using a fork.

6. Whisk the egg white until it is stiff, then fold this carefully and thoroughly into the mango mixture. Sweeten with liquid sweetener to taste, if used.

7. Return the mango mixture to the deep freeze, and freeze until completely set.

8. To serve, remove from the deep freeze 10 minutes before required, then spoon into individual serving dishes.

Step 2 Purée the mango flesh in a liquidiser or food processor, until it is smooth.

Step 5 Break up the ice crystals which have formed in the mango mixture into small pieces using the back of a fork.

Cook's Notes

Time
Preparation takes about 15 minutes, plus freezing time.

Variation
Use any other favourite fruit in place of the mango.

Serving Idea
Serve with fresh fruit.

HEALTHY COOKING

SUGAR FREE

FOR THE SWEET ALTERNATIVE

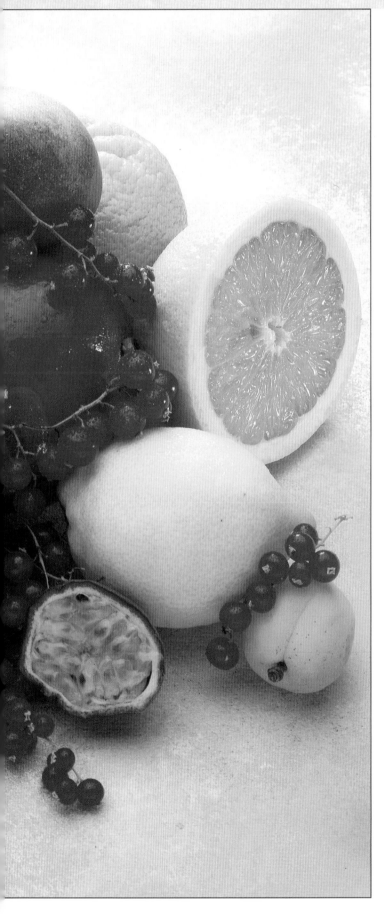

Introduction

In today's health-conscious atmosphere we are all becoming more aware of the disadvantages of a high sugar intake – increasing levels of obesity and tooth decay are the most obvious results of just such a diet. We now eat as much sugar in two weeks as people of two centuries ago did in one year, yet as we live less active lives, we actually require less energy than our forefathers.

There are many misconceptions about the properties of sugar. Contrary to what many people believe, sugar does not contain any nutrients and all types of sugar, whether white or brown, or in the form of honey or maple syrup, have the same calorific value. Sugar, or sucrose to give it its technical name, is a complex carbohydrate made up of two simple sugars. The first, fructose, is the sweetest and is found naturally in fruits. The second, glucose, is formed by the body during the digestion of plants and vegetables. Sugars are all digested in the same way: the sugar is broken down into glucose, which then travels around in the blood as energy; if this energy isn't used, it is stored as fat reserves.

By eating naturally sweet foods we can educate our palates to prefer these to over-sweet, sugared foods. The extra chewing needed will also produce more saliva to clean away the sugary film from the teeth and help prevent decay. As naturally sweet foods also take longer to digest, our bodies will not experience the short-lived artificial 'highs' that refined sugars produce.

Unfortunately, it is not always possible to leave sugar out of recipes as it can be vital for a dish's preservation or structure. However, cutting down our sugar intake gradually and avoiding those processed foods which contain sugar is a big step towards a healthier diet. In addition, eating more naturally sweet foods containing fructose, such as strawberries, not only reduces calorie intake but also provides some nutritional benefits from the food, including vitamins and fibre.

Switching to a healthier diet does not mean sacrificing taste but rather replacing refined sugars with more natural sugars and sweet fruits. The recipes in this book do just that, providing a varied selection of wholesome dishes that are delicious too!

SERVES 6-8

SULTANA SODA BREAD

Sultanas add a natural sweetness which makes this bread ideal for serving as a tea-time treat.

450g/1lb plain white flour
5ml/1 tsp salt
5ml/1 tsp bicarbonate of soda
5ml/1 tsp cream of tartar
280ml/½ pint sour milk
120g/4oz sultanas

1. Sift together the flour, salt, bicarbonate of soda and cream of tartar in a mixing bowl.

2. Add the sultanas and mix into the flour quickly, making a slight well in the centre of the flour as you do so.

3. Pour the milk into the well in the flour, and mix with a round bladed knife to form a firm, but not too stiff dough.

4. Turn the dough onto a lightly floured board, and knead quickly to bring all the ingredients together well.

5. Shape the dough into a round, and flatten it slightly with the palm of your hand.

6. Place the dough round on a lightly greased and floured baking sheet. Cut a deep cross into the top of the dough with a sharp knife.

7. Bake the dough in a preheated oven 200°C/400°F/ Gas Mark 6 for 25 minutes.

8. After this time, turn the loaf upside down on the tray and return to the oven for a further 10 minutes to dry out completely.

9. Wrap the baked loaf in a damp cloth, and place on a wire rack to cool completely.

Step 6 Cut a deep cross into the top of the bread dough using a sharp knife.

Step 8 Turn the loaf upside down on the baking tray before returning to the oven for a further 10 minutes.

Cook's Notes

Time
Preparation takes 15 minutes, cooking takes 35 minutes.

Preparation
To test that the loaf is completely cooked, tap the base with your fingers and if it sounds hollow it is ready.

Cook's Tip
If you do not have sour milk, use fresh milk with 15ml/1 tbsp of natural yogurt added.

Variation
Use wholemeal flour instead of the white flour in this recipe.

Freezing
This bread freezes well.

SERVES 10-12

FRUIT SCONES

Scones are always a firm favourite and do not need any added sugar when made with plenty of fruit.

225g/8oz plain flour
5ml/1 tsp cream of tartar
2.5ml/½ tsp bicarbonate of soda
1.25ml/¼ tsp salt
45g/1½oz butter
75g/3oz sultanas
15g/½oz sunflower seeds
15g/½oz fresh stem ginger
2 eggs
Extra milk for blending
Beaten egg, for glaze

Step 9 Roll out the dough to no less than 1.25cm/½-inch thick.

Step 2 Rub the butter into the sieved flour until the mixture resembles fine breadcrumbs.

1. Mix the flour, cream of tartar, bicarbonate of soda and salt together, and sieve it twice through a metal sieve to aerate completely.

2. Put the sieved flour into a large bowl, and rub in the butter until the mixture resembles fine breadcrumbs.

3. Stir the sultanas and the sunflower seeds into the flour and butter mixture.

4. Peel the ginger, and cut or grate it into very small pieces.

5. Using a pestle and mortar or the handle of a large knife, crush the ginger until it becomes a paste.

6. Put the ginger into a small bowl along with the eggs, and beat together with a fork until they are evenly blended.

7. Add the beaten eggs and ginger to the flour and sultana mixture, mixing well to form a soft dough, and adding a little extra milk if the dough is too stiff.

8. Lightly flour a work surface. Turn out the dough and knead it lightly until it becomes smooth.

9. Roll the dough out to approximately 1.25cm/½-inch thick.

10. Cut the dough into 5cm/2-inch rounds using a biscuit cutter.

11. Place the scones on a greased baking sheet, and brush each one with the extra beaten egg. Bake in a pre-heated oven 200°C/400°F/Gas Mark 6 for 10-15 minutes, or until golden brown and well risen.

Cook's Notes

Time
Preparation takes approximately 15 minutes, cooking takes 10-15 minutes.

Preparation
Do not roll the dough out too thinly, otherwise the scones will not rise properly.

Variation
Use other combinations of dried fruit and nuts, or seeds, in place of the sultanas and sunflower seeds in this recipe.

SERVES 6-8

SUGAR-FREE FRUIT CAKE

There is no need for sugar in a recipe rich in the natural sweetness of dried fruits.

560g/1¼lbs plain flour
2.5ml/½ tsp bicarbonate of soda
5ml/1 tsp mixed spice
5ml/1 tsp ground nutmeg
225g/8oz butter
340g/12oz raisins
225g/8oz currants
340g/12oz sultanas
120g/4oz mixed peel
280ml/½ pint Guinness, or stout
3 eggs

Step 9 The cake batter should drop easily into the prepared tin, but not be too runny, or it will seep around the lining paper.

1. Sift the flour, bicarbonate of soda, mixed spice and nutmeg into a large bowl, using a metal sieve.

2. Cut the butter into small dice, and rub into the flour using the fingertips, until the mixture resembles fine breadcrumbs.

3. Add all the fruit to the flour and mix well to distribute evenly.

4. Push the flour and fruit mixture away from the centre of the bowl to form a slight well.

5. Put the Guinness and the eggs into a large jug and whisk together thoroughly, until frothy.

6. Pour the Guinness and eggs into the well in the centre of the flour mixture.

7. Mix the Guinness and eggs together to form a soft batter, using a round bladed knife.

8. Grease and line a 22.5cm/9-inch round cake tin with greaseproof paper.

9. Pour the cake batter into the tin and bake in the centre of a preheated oven 160°C/325°F/Gas Mark 3 for 2 hours. Reduce the temperature to 140°C/275°F/Gas Mark 1 after the first hour if the cake appears to be cooking too quickly.

10. Test the cake with a skewer to see when it is done. If it is cooked, the skewer will come out clean. Turn the cake onto a wire rack, remove the lining paper and cool it completely before storing in an airtight tin for 2-3 days, before serving.

Cook's Notes

 Time
Preparation takes approximately 30 minutes, cooking takes 2 hours.

Variation
Use wholemeal flour in place of the white flour in this recipe, cider instead of Guinness, and grated apple instead of mixed peel.

 Preparation
If the cake is cooking too quickly, the sides will become brown and the centre of the cake will rise up into a point. If this should happen, reduce the temperature and cook at a much slower heat. Cover the top of the cake with aluminium foil to prevent it from browning further.

 Cook's Tip
The flavour of this cake really does improve if it can be kept in an airtight container for a few days before using.

 Freezing
This cake freezes very well for up to 3 months.

SERVES 4-6

GRIDDLE SCONES

The whole fun of these cakes is that they can be eaten directly from the pan in which they are cooked. So gather family and friends around you for a traditional tea-time treat.

120g/4oz self-raising flour
Pinch salt
45g/1½oz butter or margarine
120g/4oz currants
2.5ml/½ tsp ground nutmeg
1 egg
90ml/3 fl oz milk

Step 1 Rub the butter into the flour with your fingertips, until the mixture resembles fine breadcrumbs.

Step 4 Using a wooden spoon, mix the egg and flour mixture into the flour, stirring from the centre of the bowl and drawing the flour in from the sides to form a smooth, thick batter.

Step 6 Fry tablespoons of the batter in a hot pan until the undersides have browned lightly and the tops are just set.

1. Mix the flour and salt together, and rub in the butter until the mixture resembles fine breadcrumbs.

2. Stir in the currants and the nutmeg, then push the mixture gently to the sides of the bowl to form a well in the centre.

3. Beat together the egg and the milk, and pour the into the well in the centre of the flour.

4. Using a wooden spoon, mix the egg and milk mixture into the flour, stirring from the centre of the bowl and drawing the flour in from the sides to form a smooth, thick batter.

5. Heat a heavy-based frying pan on top of a moderate heat, and grease with a little butter or oil.

6. Drop tablespoons of the batter into the hot pan, and cook for 2-3 minutes, or until the bases are set and have turned golden brown.

7. Turn the scones over and cook on the other side in the same way.

8. Serve from the pan with sugar-free preserves.

Cook's Notes

Time
Preparation takes 15 minutes, cooking takes about 4 minutes per scone.

Preparation
If the batter is too thick, add a little extra milk until it becomes a soft dropping consistency.

Freezing
These scones freeze well, and can be re-heated by wrapping in a clean tea towel and standing in a warm oven until they are heated through.

SERVES 6-8
FRUIT LOAF

There is no need to add sugar to this recipe as the easy-blend yeast will work on the natural sugars provided by the fruit.

450g/1lb strong plain flour
2.5ml/½ tsp cinnamon
2.5ml/½ tsp nutmeg
2.5ml/½ tsp salt
225g/8oz sultanas
225g/8oz currants
60g/2oz cut mixed peel
1 sachet of easy blend yeast
30ml/2 tbsps vegetable oil
280ml/½ pint lukewarm milk
1 large egg

1. Put the flour, spices and salt into a large mixing bowl.

2. Stir in the sultanas, currants and mixed peel, mixing well to distribute the fruit evenly.

3. Sprinkle over the sachet of yeast, and mix this directly into the dry ingredients.

4. Put the oil, milk and egg into a large jug, and beat together with a fork until the egg is broken up evenly. Add the mixture to the flour, and mix together, stirring until the batter becomes stiff and elastic.

5. Turn the batter onto a lightly floured board, and knead until smooth – approximately 10 minutes.

6. Return the batter to the bowl and cover with a damp cloth or a piece of clingfilm. Leave the batter in a warm place for about 1 hour to allow the dough to rise.

7. After this time, the dough should be approximately double its original size.

8. Punch the dough down to remove the air, and turn it out once again onto the lightly floured surface.

9. Continue kneading the dough for approximately 5 minutes, then cut in two.

Step 4 Mix the milk mixture into the flour and yeast mixture, stirring until a soft, but elastic, dough is formed.

Step 10 Shape the pieces of dough to fit into 2 lightly greased, or non-stick loaf tins.

10. Shape each piece of dough to fit 2 x 17.5cm/7-inch non-stick loaf tins. Cover each tin lightly with clingfilm or a damp cloth, and leave once again in a warm place until the loaves have risen to double their size.

11. Bake the loaves for 30-40 minutes in the centre of a preheated oven 200°C/400°F/Gas Mark 6, removing the loaves from the oven after 20 minutes, and brushing the surfaces with a little milk.

12. To test if the loaves are cooked, turn out of the tins and tap the bases with your knuckles, if it sounds hollow, the loaves are ready.

13. Serve warm, or allow to cool and serve sliced, with butter.

Cook's Notes

 Time
Preparation takes approximately 2 hours, cooking takes 40 minutes.

 Variation
Use any combination of your favourite dried fruits in this recipe.

 Freezing
This recipe freezes well for up to 2 months.

MAKES 10

FRUIT TRUFFLES

These delicious little cakes get all the sweetness they require from fresh bananas.

2 bananas
Juice ½ orange
Finely grated rind 1 orange
150g/5oz ground almonds
30g/1oz blanched almonds
15ml/1 tbsp plain cocoa

1. Chop the bananas into a large bowl and using a potato masher, mash them until they are smooth.

2. Mix in the orange juice and rind.

3. Stir in the ground almonds, mixing well to blend evenly. Place the mixture in a refrigerator and chill for approximately 30 minutes.

4. Using a sharp knife, finely chop the blanched almonds into small pieces.

5. Mix the chopped almonds into the cocoa powder, and place on a flat plate.

Step 1 Mash the bananas to a smooth pulp using a potato masher.

Step 7 Roll the banana mixture into 10 even-sized balls, using lightly floured hands.

Step 8 Cover each banana truffle with an even coating of chopped nuts and cocoa, pressing this gently onto the surface to ensure it stays in place.

6. Remove the banana mixture from the refrigerator, and divide into 10 portions.

7. Roll each portion into a small ball, using lightly floured hands.

8. Roll each ball into the cocoa and almond mixture, rolling each one evenly to give a good coating. Press gently before placing into a small paper cases, and chilling once again.

Cook's Notes

Time
Preparation takes approximately 25 minutes, plus chilling time.

Cook's Tip
Do not keep these delicious sweets for long after they have been made, or the banana will go brown and wet.

Variation
Use walnuts in place of almonds in this recipe.

MAKES 900g/2lbs

COCONUT CHUTNEY

This unusual chutney is a welcome change from the more common fruit chutneys.

2 fresh coconuts
1.25cm/½-inch piece fresh root ginger
2 green chillies
5ml/1 tsp cumin seed
60ml/4 tbsps finely chopped fresh coriander leaves
45ml/3 tbsps lemon juice
2.5ml/½ tsp salt

1. Crack the coconuts in half, and carefully pour out and reserve the milk.

2. Remove the coconut flesh from inside the shells, and peel off the brown outer skin.

3. Chop the peeled coconut into small pieces.

4. Peel the root ginger and finely chop or grate the flesh.

5. Cut the green chillies in half, remove and discard the seeds, and finely chop the outer flesh.

6. Put the coconut, ginger, chillies, cumin seeds, coriander, lemon and salt into a liquidiser or food processor, and blend with enough coconut milk to produce a thick creamy chutney.

7. Pour the mixture into pots and seal well.

8. Keep in a refrigerator and use within 2-3 weeks.

Step 4 Finely chop or grate the peeled root ginger.

Step 2 Peel away the brown skin from the flesh of the coconut using a sharp knife.

Step 6 Blend the chutney ingredients with coconut milk in a liquidiser or food processor until it is thick and creamy.

Cook's Notes

Time
Preparation takes approximately 20 minutes.

Freezing
This recipe freezes well.

Preparation
If you do not have a liquidiser or a food processor, the coconut and other ingredients can be grated, but this will not produce such a smooth textured chutney.

Serving Idea
This chutney is delicious served with cold meats, curries, or in sandwiches.

MAKES APPROXIMATELY 2kgs/5lbs

FRUIT CHUTNEY

The use of canned fruit means that this delicious chutney can be prepared at any time of the year.

425g/15oz can pears in natural juice
425g/15oz can peach slices in natural juice
350g/12oz can pineapple chunks in natural juice
225g/8oz can prunes in natural juice
450g/1lb plums
4 cooking apples
120g/4oz fresh dates
120g/4oz ready-to-use dried apricots
2.5cm/1-inch piece fresh root ginger, peeled and thinly sliced
120g/4oz blanched almonds
120g/4oz cashew nuts
60ml/4 tbsps malt vinegar
2.5ml/½ tsp ground cloves
5ml/1 tsp chilli powder
5cm/2-inch piece cinnamon stick
2 bananas, peeled and sliced

1. Remove the stones from the plums and chop the flesh into fairly large pieces.

2. Drain the fruit juices from the cans of fruit, and set aside. Chop the fruit into large pieces.

3. Cut the apples into four and remove the cores, but do not peel.

4. Finely slice the apple and mix this with the chopped fruit in a large saucepan.

5. Stone the fresh dates, and chop the dates and the dried apricots into small pieces. Add the apricots and dates to the saucepan of fruit, along with all the remaining ingredients, except for the reserved juice.

6. Pour over enough of the reserved juice to just cover the fruit.

7. Cover the pan, and bring the chutney to the boil. Reduce the heat and simmer for 15-20 minutes.

8. Remove the lid of the pan and stir the chutney well. Add a little extra juice if required, and continue cooking for a further 10 minutes, uncovered, stirring occasionally to prevent the mixture from burning.

9. When the chutney is thick and most of the liquid has evaporated, divide it between clean warm glass jars. Cover with waxed paper and a tight fitting lid, then store for up to 3 months in a refrigerator.

Step 1 Cut the plums in half and carefully remove the stones. Chop the flesh into fairly large pieces.

Step 9 When cooked, the chutney should be thick and most of the liquid should have evaporated.

Cook's Notes

Time
Preparation takes approximately 15 minutes, cooking takes 30 minutes.

Serving Idea
Serve with cold meats, cheeses, or in sandwiches.

Cook's Tip
Check that the chutney does not stick to the base of the pan, by stirring occasionally whilst it is cooking.

Variation
If you cannot get fresh plums, try using mangoes or apricots.

Freezing
This recipe will freeze well.

MAKES APPROXIMATELY 900g/2lbs

SUGAR FREE MINCEMEAT

Not only is this recipe free from refined sugar, it is also completely fat free, making it extremely healthy.

3 large red eating apples
225g/8oz raisins
225g/8oz currants
225g/8oz sultanas
120g/4oz fresh dates
60g/2oz blanched almonds
140ml/¼ pint brandy or sherry

Step 3 Blend the pitted dates with the nuts and brandy, or sherry, until they are fairly coarsely chopped.

Step 1 Quarter the apples, remove the cores and chop the flesh roughly.

Step 4 Mix the date mixture with the apple and fruit mixture, stirring well to blend evenly.

1. Quarter the apples, remove the cores and chop the apple flesh.

2. Put the apples into a liquidiser or food processor, along with the raisins, currants and sultanas. Chop the fruit finely, then transfer to a large mixing bowl.

3. Carefully remove the stones from the dates and put the fruit into a food processor or liquidiser, along with the nuts

and the brandy or sherry. Process until the dates and nuts are roughly chopped.

4. Mix the date mixture into the apple and dried fruit mixture, stirring well to blend all ingredients thoroughly.

5. Divide the mixture between 2-3 clean glass jars, then cover and allow to stand for up to 3 weeks before using.

Cook's Notes

Time
Preparation takes approximately 20 minutes.

Serving Idea
Use in minced pies or apple pie as a natural sweetener.

Freezing
This recipe will freeze, but should be stirred well when thawed to distribute the alcohol evenly.

MAKES 450ml/¾ pint

CHOCOLATE BUTTER SAUCE

The sugar-free (diabetic) chocolate used in this recipe is readily available in most chemists and health food shops.

250ml/8 fl oz water
225g/8oz plain sugar-free chocolate, chopped
105g/3½oz butter, cut into small pieces
15ml/1 tbsp brandy

Step 1 Melt the chocolate in the water over a low heat, stirring until the mixture is smooth.

1. Put the water and the chocolate into a saucepan, and heat over a low heat, stirring until the chocolate has melted.

2. Remove the melted chocolate and water from the heat and slowly stir in the butter, piece by piece, until the mixture becomes thick and glossy.

3. Whisk the brandy into the butter sauce and spoon into an attractive serving dish. This sauce can be served hot or cold.

Step 2 Drop the butter into the melted chocolate, piece by piece, stirring well until it has melted.

Step 3 Beat the brandy into the sauce, whisking until it is thick and glossy.

Cook's Notes

Time
Preparation takes approximately 5 minutes, cooking takes 10 minutes.

Preparation
After melting the chocolate and water together, the mixture should be smooth, with no lumps in it.

Serving Idea
Serve with fresh fruit or pancakes.

Watchpoint
Do not heat the chocolate and water too rapidly or the mixture will curdle.

MAKES 250ml/8 fl oz

MOCHA SAUCE

*This unusual coffee chocolate sauce gets its sweetness from the delightfully
tangy apricot purée.*

120g/4oz plain sugar-free chocolate
45ml/3 tbsps very strong black coffee
120ml/4 fl oz double cream
120ml/4 fl oz thick apricot purée (see separate recipe)

Step 3 Stir the double cream into the chocolate and coffee mixture, mixing well to blend evenly.

Step 2 Melt the chocolate and coffee together in a bowl which is standing over a saucepan of hot water.

2. Put the chocolate and the coffee into a large bowl, and stand the bowl over a saucepan half filled with simmering water. Remove the saucepan and the bowl from the heat, and stir the chocolate gently until it has melted.

3. Add the double cream to the melted chocolate, mixing well to blend evenly.

1. Grate the chocolate, or chop it into small pieces with a sharp knife.

4. Stir in the apricot purée, transfer the chocolate sauce to a serving dish and chill thoroughly.

Cook's Notes

 Time
Preparation takes approximately 5 minutes, cooking takes 15 minutes.

 Serving Idea
Serve this delicious sauce with fruit or pancakes.

 Watchpoint
Take great care not to cook the chocolate and the coffee together too quickly, or the chocolate will separate and curdle.

MAKES APPROXIMATELY 280ml/½ pint

APRICOT PURÉE

This delicious tangy sauce is made with canned apricots in natural juice, thus making use of the natural sweetness of fruit sugars.

425g/15oz can apricot halves in natural juice
Juice and rind 1 lime
30ml/2 tbsps apricot brandy (optional)

1. Purée the apricots in their juice, using a liquidiser or food processor.

2. Put the apricot purée into a small saucepan.

3. Stir the lime juice and rind into the apricot mixture, and heat over a low temperature until it begins to boil.

4. Continue simmering over a low temperature until the sauce is thick and liquid has reduced.

Step 1 Purée the apricots in a liquidiser or food processor until they are smooth.

Step 3 Stir the lime juice and rind into the fruit purée, mixing well to blend evenly.

Step 4 Cook the apricot mixture over a low heat until the sauce has thickened and the liquid has evaporated.

5. Cool the purée in a refrigerator until required, and serve after stirring in the apricot brandy.

Cook's Notes

Time
Preparation takes 2 minutes, cooking takes 5 minutes.

Variation
Use canned pears or prunes in place of the apricots in this recipe.

Serving Idea
Serve with pancakes, or fresh fruit.

SERVES 10-12

APPLE SAUCE

This sauce is extremely versatile and can be used as an accompaniment to meats or fish, as well as being included in ingredients for desserts.

900g/2lbs cooking apples
280ml/½ pint apple juice
1.25ml/¼ tsp ground cloves
Finely pared rind ½ orange

1. Wash the apples and cut away any bruised or discoloured pieces. Cut the fruit into large pieces.

2. Put the chopped fruit into a large pan, along with the apple juice, ground cloves and the orange rind. Bring to the boil and simmer until most of the liquid has evaporated and the fruit has softened.

3. Cool the cooked apples.

4. Put the cooled apples into a nylon sieve over a large bowl, and press through using the back of a wooden spoon, to remove all skin, pips and cores.

5. Put the apple purée into cartons or jars, and store or freeze until required.

6. Serve in a bowl and decorate with a sprig of mint.

Step 1 Wash the apples and cut away any bruising or discoloured pieces.

Step 2 Cook the apples in the fruit juice until the liquid has reduced, and the fruit is soft and pulpy.

Step 4 Press the cooled fruit through a nylon sieve into a bowl, using the back of a wooden spoon to push the fruit purée through and to remove the cores, skin and pips.

Cook's Notes

Time
Preparation takes approximately 30 minutes, cooking takes about 20 minutes.

Preparation
If preferred, the cooked apples can be puréed in a liquidiser or food processor before pressing through the sieve to remove the skins and cores.

Variation
Use cinnamon instead of the cloves in this recipe.

Freezing
This sauce can be frozen for up to 4 months.

MAKES 10-12 PANCAKES

CREPES

These tasty pancakes are delicious with both sweet and tangy sauces.

120g/4oz plain flour
Pinch salt
1 egg
280ml/½ pint milk
5ml/1 tsp vegetable oil
Juice and rind of a lemon and orange

1. Sieve the flour and the salt into a large bowl. Push the flour gently towards the sides of the bowl to make a well in the centre.

2. Put the egg and the milk into a jug and beat well.

3. Gradually add the egg and milk mixture to the flour, pouring it into the centre of the bowl, and mixing gently by stirring and drawing the flour in from the sides.

4. Continue adding the egg mixture gradually and beat until all the flour has been incorporated.

5. Heat a little oil in a small frying pan, and pour in enough batter to make a thin pancake.

6. Quickly tilt and rotate the frying pan so that the batter coats the bottom of it evenly.

7. Cook the pancake over a moderate heat until the underside has turned brown and the top has set.

8. Carefully turn the pancake over and brown the other side in the same way.

9. Turn each pancake out onto greaseproof paper and keep them warm until required.

10. Serve the pancakes hot with freshly squeezed orange and lemon juice and decorate with the pared citrus rind.

Step 1 Gently push the flour towards the sides of the bowl to make a well in the centre.

Step 3 Gradually add the egg and milk to the flour, mixing from the centre of the bowl and drawing the flour into the liquid.

Step 6 Quickly tilt and rotate the frying pan so that the batter coats the bottom thinly.

Cook's Notes

Time
Preparation takes approximately 10 minutes, cooking takes about 20 minutes for all the pancakes.

Watchpoint
Do not overheat your frying pan or the base of the pancake will burn before the top has set. Also, do not attempt to turn the pancakes until the underside is properly cooked.

Freezing
Pancakes can be made in greater quantities than this recipe, and frozen until required.

MAKES 2 x 1.2LT/2 PINT PUDDINGS

CHRISTMAS PUDDING

Christmas puddings are always thought of as being sweet and heavy. Try this sugar-free recipe for a fresh tasting change.

450g/1lb mixed dried fruit
180g/6oz seedless raisins
180g/6oz stoned dates
180g/6oz stoned, ready to use prunes
45g/1½ oz blanched shredded almonds
180g/6oz fresh white breadcrumbs
180g/6oz shredded suet
180g/6oz plain flour
2.5ml/½ level tsp ground nutmeg
2.5ml/½ tsp ground cinnamon
1.25ml/¼ tsp salt
1 carrot, grated
1 cooking apple, grated
Grated rind and juice 1 orange
140ml/¼ pint brandy, or stout
1 egg

1. Put all the fruit into a mincer or food processor, and chop finely.

2. Put the chopped fruits into a large mixing bowl, add all the remaining ingredients, and mix well.

3. Grease 2 x 1.2lt/2 pint pudding basins, and divide the mixture evenly between both basins.

4. Cover the top of the puddings with a buttered circle of greaseproof paper.

5. Make a foil pudding lid by cutting a large piece of aluminium foil, and pleating it down the centre. Tie this lid securely onto the basins.

6. Stand the puddings on an up-turned saucer or trivet, in a large saucepan.

7. Add enough boiling water to the saucepans to come two thirds of the way up the side of the pudding bowls.

8. Cover the saucepans and boil the puddings for 4-5 hours, keeping the water topped up as it evaporates.

9. Remove the basins from the water and remove the covering paper.

10. Up-turn a serving plate over the puddings, and turn the whole pudding over, shaking it gently to help it drop out of the basin onto the serving plate.

11. Serve ignited with brandy, if desired.

Step 2 Mix the minced fruit together in a large bowl with all the remaining ingredients, stirring well to blend thoroughly.

Step 5 Cover the pudding with a pleated foil pudding lid, tying this down securely before boiling.

Cook's Notes

Time
Preparation takes approximately 30 minutes, cooking takes about 5 hours.

Serving Idea
Serve with brandy butter or fresh cream.

Preparation
To be at its best this pudding should be prepared at least 3 months in advance.

Cook's Tip
This pudding can be stored for up to a year. To re-heat before use, pop into a pan of simmering water and cook for 3 hours.

SERVES 4-6

COCONUT SORBET

Naturally sweet coconut milk and dark rum blend lusciously to produce a sorbet rich with the flavours of the Caribbean.

400g/14oz can coconut milk
90ml/3 fl oz mineral water
90ml/3 fl oz dark rum
2 egg whites
Liquid sweetener to taste (optional)
2 bananas, thinly sliced and brushed with lemon juice and flaked coconut, to decorate

1. Mix the coconut milk with the mineral water, rum and liquid sweetener to taste, if required. Pour into a large freezer container and put into the freezer for 1 hour, or until the sides are beginning to freeze.

2. Using a fork, break the frozen coconut mixture up into a thin slush, making sure that there are no large ice crystals left in the mixture. Return to the freezer and continue freezing for a further hour.

3. Remove the coconut mixture from the freezer, and break up as before with a fork to make a thicker slush. Return the mixture to the freezer whilst you whisk the egg whites.

4. Whisk the egg whites until they form soft peaks.

5. Remove the partially frozen coconut mixture from the freezer and make sure that it can be easily stirred.

6. Carefully fold the egg whites into the coconut mixture, mixing lightly but thoroughly to blend evenly.

Step 2 Break the crystals away from the edge of the freezer dish using a fork, and mixing well to make a thin slush.

Step 6 Fold the softly whipped egg whites into the partially frozen slush, mixing lightly but thoroughly, to blend evenly.

7. Return the sorbet to the freezer and freeze until completely set.

8. To serve, remove the sorbet from the freezer 10 minutes before it is required and break it up with a fork into large ice crystals. Pile the crystals into serving dishes and decorate with the banana and the flakes of coconut.

Cook's Notes

Time
Preparation takes approximately 20 minutes, freezing takes 2-3 hours.

Variation
Use pineapple juice in place of the rum, and serve with pineapple pieces and coconut flakes.

Preparation
Make sure that the ice crystals are not too wet when you fold in the egg whites, otherwise the mixture will separate during freezing.

Cook's Tip
Make double quantities of this sorbet, as it freezes well for up to 3 months and is ideal as a stand-by dessert.

SERVES 4-6

EXOTIC FRUIT SALAD

Mangoes are exceptionally sweet when ripe, and give this lovely fruit salad a natural tangy sweetness.

3 ripe peaches
3 kiwi fruits
1 large star fruit
120g/4oz fresh strawberries
2 well-ripened mangoes, each weighing about
   340g/12oz
Juice of half a lime
150g/5oz redcurrants
Few strawberry leaves for decoration

Step 9 Press the mango purée through a wire sieve, using a wooden spoon to remove the pips and skins from the redcurrants.

Step 5 Cut away any brown pieces from the skin of the star fruit using a sharp knife.

1. Plunge the peaches into boiling water for a few seconds, then carefully peel away the skin using a sharp knife.

2. Carefully cut the peaches in half and remove the stone.

3. Cut the peach halves into thin slices and arrange on a serving plate.

4. Cut away the peel from the kiwi fruits and slice them crosswise to show their attractive colour.

5. Trim away any dark pieces from the skin of the star fruit, cut the flesh into thin slices, and remove any small pips you may find.

6. Leave the green stems on the strawberries and cut them in half lengthways. Arrange all the prepared fruit on the serving platter with the peaches.

7. Peel the mango and chop away the flesh from the large inner stone.

8. Put the chopped mango flesh into a liquidiser or food processor, along with the lime juice and half of the redcurrants.

9. Purée the mixture until smooth, then press the purée through a nylon sieve to remove the redcurrant skins and pips.

10. Sprinkle the remaining redcurrants over the fruit on the serving platter, removing any hard stems or leaves as you do so.

11. Pour the fruit purée evenly over the fruit salad, and chill for at least 1 hour before serving, decorated with the strawberry leaves.

Cook's Notes

Time
Preparation takes approximately 25 minutes, plus 1 hour chilling time.

Variation
Use any combination of your favourite fruits in the fruit salad, but do not change the mango purée.

Preparation
If you do not have a liquidiser or food processor, a really ripe mango will rub easily through a wire sieve and will not need to be reduced to a purée first.

Cook's Tip
Add 45ml/3 tbsps rum to the mango purée to give extra flavour for a special occasion.

SERVES 6

RASPBERRY SOUFFLÉ

This light dessert is the perfect finale for a dinner party.

450g/1lb raspberries
Liquid sweetener to taste
15g/½oz gelatin
140ml/¼ pint hot water
4 eggs, separated
280ml/½ pint double cream

Step 1 Tie a sheet of greaseproof paper around the souffle dish, to form a collar rising above the rim of the dish.

1. Prepare a 15cm/6-inch souffle dish by tightly tying a lightly oiled sheet of greaseproof paper carefully around the outside edge of the souffle dish, allowing it to stand approximately 10cm/4 inches above the rim of the dish.

2. Reserve a few of the raspberries for decoration, and purée the remainder using a liquidiser or food processor.

3. Rub the puréed raspberries through a nylon sieve to remove the hard pips.

4. Sweeten the smooth raspberry purée with the liquid sweetener and set aside.

5. Dissolve the gelatin in the hot water, stirring gently until it is completely dissolved and the liquid is clear.

6. Allow the gelatin to cool slightly and then beat it into the raspberry purée along with the egg yolks, mixing until all ingredients are well blended. Chill in the refrigerator until partially set.

7. Whisk the egg whites until they form soft peaks.

8. Lightly whip half of the double cream until it is softly stiff.

9. Remove the partially set raspberry mixture from the refrigerator, and carefully fold in the cream and the egg

Step 3 Press the raspberry purée through a metal sieve, to remove the pips.

whites, blending lightly but thoroughly until the mixture is smooth.

10. Turn the prepared souffle mixture into the dish, allowing it to rise about 2.5cm/1 inch above the rim of the dish inside the paper collar. Allow to set in the refrigerator.

11. When completely set, remove the collar carefully and decorate the souffle with the remaining whipped cream and the reserved raspberries.

Cook's Notes

Time
Preparation takes approximately 40 minutes, plus chilling time.

Watchpoint
Do not add the gelatin to boiling water, or this will impair its setting qualities.

Preparation
Take great care not to over-mix the souffle mixture when adding the egg whites, or there will not be enough to rise up over the rim of the dish inside the collar.

Variation
Use strawberries, or any other favourite fresh fruit in place of the raspberries in this recipe.

Freezing
Cold souffles freeze very well for up to 6 weeks, but should be decorated after they have thawed.

SERVES 4

PASSION FRUIT ICE CREAM

Fruit ice creams are actually more refreshing without added sugar, but if you must have added sweetness use liquid sweetener.

6 passion fruits
280ml/½ pint natural yogurt
2 egg yolks
Liquid sweetener to taste (optional)
1-2 passion fruits, halved and scooped for decoration

Step 1 Cut the 6 passion fruits in half and scoop all the centre pulp into a bowl using a small spoon.

Step 2 Beat together the yogurt, egg yolks and passion fruit pulp until they are well blended.

Step 4 Break up the partially frozen passion fruit ice cream using a fork, and mixing until a smooth slush is formed.

1. Halve the 6 passion fruits, and scoop out all the centre pulp into a bowl.

2. Add the yogurt and egg yolks to the passion fruit pulp, and mix together well, adding liquid sweetener to taste, if desired.

3. Pour the passion fruit mixture into a shallow container, and freeze until partially set – approximately 1 hour.

4. Break the ice crystals in the partially set passion fruit mixture using a fork, and mixing well until they form a smooth slush.

5. Return the ice cream to the freezer and freeze until completely firm.

6. To serve, remove the ice cream from the freezer for 10 minutes, then pile scoops of ice cream into stemmed glasses, and serve with passion fruit pulp poured over each portion.

Cook's Notes

Time
Preparation takes approximately 20 minutes, plus freezing time.

Variation
Add 30ml/2 tbsps rum or brandy to the ice cream mixture before freezing.

Watchpoint
This ice cream goes extremely hard when frozen, so it is important to remember to remove it from the freezer 10 minutes before serving.

SERVES 4

ALMOND-STUFFED FIGS

Fresh figs are now easily available from most major supermarkets and good greengrocers. When ripe, they go a luscious purple black and are soft to the touch.

4 large ripe figs
60ml/4 tbsps ground almonds
30ml/2 tbsps orange juice
30ml/2 tbsps finely chopped dried apricots
60ml/4 tbsps natural yogurt
Finely grated rind ½ orange
Wedges of figs and mint, or strawberry leaves for decoration

Step 2 Ease the four sections of each fig outwards to form a flower shape.

Step 1 Carefully cut a cross into each fig, making sure that you do not cut right through down to the base.

Step 4 Divide the almond mixture evenly between the four figs, and press it into the centre of each one.

1. Cut each fig into four quarters using a sharp knife, and taking care not to cut right down through the base.

2. Ease the four sections of each fig outward to form a flower shape.

3. Put the ground almonds, orange juice and chopped apricots into a small bowl and mix together thoroughly.

4. Divide this mixture into four, and press it into the centre

of each fig.

5. For the sauce, mix the yogurt with the orange rind, and thin it down with just a little water, or orange juice.

6. Spoon a small pool of orange yogurt onto each of four plates, and sit a stuffed fig into the centre of each pool. Decorate with the additional wedges of fig, and the mint or strawberry leaves.

Cook's Notes

 Time
Preparation takes approximately 25 minutes.

 Variation
Use peach halves instead of the figs in this recipe.

 Watchpoint
Do not add too much water or orange juice to the sauce, or it will become too thin.

SERVES 6

CHERRY COMPÔTE

Black cherries and apple juice combine perfectly in this tasty dessert.

675g/1½lbs fresh black cherries
430ml/¾ pint apple or grape juice
7.5ml/1½ tsps finely grated lemon rind
38ml/2½ tbsps cornflour or arrowroot
45ml/3 tbsps brandy (optional)

1. Remove the stones from the cherries, using a cherry stoner or the rounded end of a potato peeler.

2. Put the pitted cherries into a saucepan, along with the apple or grape juice and the lemon rind. Bring to the boil over a moderate heat, then simmer for 10 minutes, or until the cherries are gently poached.

3. Remove the cherries from the juice with a slotted spoon, leaving the juice in the saucepan. Arrange the cherries in a serving bowl.

4. Blend the cornflour with 5 tbsps of the cherry juice.

5. Add the blended cornflour or arrowroot to the cherry juice in the pan, and bring to the boil stirring constantly until the sauce has thickened. Stir in the brandy if used.

6. Pour the thickened cherry sauce over the cherries in the bowl, and chill well before serving.

Step 1 Remove the stones from the cherries using a cherry stoner or the rounded end of a potato peeler.

Step 4 Blend cornflour or arrowroot with 5 tbsps of the cherry juice.

Step 5 Bring the cherry juice and blended cornflour or arrowroot, slowly to the boil, stirring all the time until the sauce thickens and clears.

Cook's Notes

 Time
Preparation takes 15-20 minutes, cooking takes about 5 minutes plus chilling time.

 Cook's Tip
Arrowroot will produce a clearer sauce than cornflour.

 Variation
Use apricots instead of cherries in this recipe.

 Freezing
This recipe freezes well.

SERVES 4-6

ORANGE AND APRICOT MOUSSE

This delicious light mousse makes an ideal end to any meal.

2 oranges
3 x 400g/14oz cans of apricots in natural juice, drained
Artificial sweetener to taste (optional)
20g/¾oz powdered gelatin
140ml/¼ pint natural yogurt
2 egg whites
Extra orange rind to decorate

1. Finely grate the rind from half of one orange using a fine grater.

2. Cut all the oranges in half and squeeze out the juice.

3. Put the drained apricots, all but 45ml/3 tbsps of the orange juice, and the orange rind into a liquidiser or food processor, and purée until smooth. Pour into a large bowl and set aside.

4. Put the 45ml/3 tbsps of orange juice into a small pan and heat gently, but do not boil.

5. Sprinkle the gelatin over the warm orange juice, and allow to stand until dissolved and clear.

6. Stir the gelatin mixture into the apricot purée, along with the natural yogurt, mixing well to blend evenly. Put in a refrigerator for about 30 minutes until almost set.

7. Whisk the egg whites until they form soft peaks.

8. Fold the whisked egg whites lightly, but thoroughly, into the partially set apricot mixture.

9. Divide the fruit mousse evenly into serving glasses and chill until completely set.

Step 3 Purée the orange juice, rind and apricots together in a liquidiser or food processor until smooth.

Step 6 Allow the fruit purée and gelatin to chill in a refrigerator until it is just beginning to set.

Step 8 Fold the egg whites carefully, but thoroughly, into the thickening fruit mixture, taking care not to over mix and lose the air in the egg whites.

Cook's Notes

 Time
Preparation takes 30-35 minutes, plus chilling time.

 Variation
Use strawberries or peaches in place of the apricots.

 Serving Idea
Serve decorated with twisted strips of orange peel and a crisp biscuit if liked.

SERVES 6

BAKED APPLES IN OVERCOATS

Pastry sweetened with cinnamon and spices combines with a rich fruit filling to make this warming winter dessert.

340g/12oz plain flour
1.25ml/¼ tsp salt
1.25ml/¼ tsp cinnamon
1.25ml/¼ tsp ground nutmeg
180g/6oz butter
75-105ml/5-7 tbsps iced water
6 medium-sized dessert apples
6 prunes, stoned
6 dried apricots
30ml/2 tbsps raisins
1 egg, beaten to glaze
Fresh cream to serve
Fresh mint to serve

1. Sift the flour, salt and spices into a large bowl.

2. Cut the butter into dice and rub into the flour until the mixture resembles fine breadcrumbs.

3. Mix in enough water to produce a smooth pliable dough.

4. Divide the dough into six pieces and roll out into a square approximately 20cm/8 inches.

5. Peel the apples with a sharp knife and carefully remove the centre cores with an apple corer.

6. Chop the prunes and the apricots and mix these with the raisins.

Step 8 Draw the sides of the pastry square up and over each apple, sealing the edges well with a little water.

7. Place one prepared apple into the centre of each pastry square, and fill the cavities with equal amounts of the dried fruit mixture.

8. Brush the edges of each square with a little water, and draw them up and around the sides of the apples, sealing them well with a little water and trimming off any excess pastry to give a neat finish.

9. Roll out the pastry trimmings, cut into decorative leaves and stick the leaves onto each apple for decoration.

10. Glaze each pastry apple with the beaten egg and place on a lightly greased baking sheet.

11. Bake the apples in a preheated oven 170°C/350°F/Gas Mark 4 for 20-25 minutes, or until golden brown.

12. Serve hot with the fresh cream and sprigs of fresh mint.

Cook's Notes

 Time
Preparation takes approximately 30 minutes, cooking time takes 20-25 minutes.

 Cook's Tip
For an extra rich pastry, use 1 egg yolk and half the amount of water in this recipe.

 Variation
Use pears instead of apples in this recipe.

 Freezing
These apples freeze well after baking and should be thawed, then re-heated, before eating.

SERVES 6

ALMOND-YOGURT SHAKE

This healthy, sugar-free yogurt shake has a slightly salty, but refreshing flavour.

380ml/⅔ pint water
430ml/¾ pint natural yogurt
10ml/2 tsps lemon juice
30ml/2 tbsps ground almonds
1.25ml/¼ tsp saffron strands
10ml/2 tsps rose water
1.25ml/¼ tsp salt

1. Lightly moisten the rims of six tumblers with a little water or lightly whipped egg white. Spread a thin layer of salt onto a saucer and dip the moistened rims into it to coat lightly.

2. Put half of the water into a liquidiser and add the yogurt, lemon juice, almonds, saffron and rose water. Blend until smooth.

3. Mix in the remaining water and the salt.

Step 1 Lightly moisten the rims of six tumblers with a little water or lightly whipped egg white. Spread a thin layer of salt onto a saucer and dip the moistened rims into it to coat lightly.

4. Measure 570ml/1 pint of ice cubes into a measuring jug.

5. Pour the yogurt mixture from the liquidiser into another large jug.

6. Put half of the ice into the liquidiser and pour over half of the yogurt and saffron mixture. Blend to a thick slush, then repeat with the remaining ice and yogurt mixture. Serve in the prepared tumblers.

Step 2 Blend the water, yogurt, lemon juice, almonds, saffron and rose water in a liquidiser or food processor, until smooth.

Step 6 Blend half of the ice with half of the liquid in the liquidiser until it forms a smooth slush.

Cook's Notes

Time
Preparation takes 10 minutes.

Cook's Tip
If you haven't got a liquidiser or food processor, use a rolling pin to crush the ice.

Variation
Use the juice of ½ an orange in place of the lemon juice in this recipe.

SERVES 6

KIWI AND PINEAPPLE SHAKE

Sugar-free lemonade is easily available in supermarkets, and adds a tangy fizz to this delicious fruity drink.

240ml/8 fl oz pineapple juice
3 kiwi fruits
280ml/10 fl oz natural yogurt
1 lemon
Liquid sweetener to taste
430ml/¾ pint ice cubes
280ml/½ pint sugar-free lemonade
1 kiwi fruit for decoration

Step 1 Purée the pineapple juice and kiwi fruits together in a liquidiser or food processor, until smooth.

1. Carefully peel the 3 kiwi fruits and roughly chop the flesh. Put the kiwi flesh into a food processor or liquidiser, along with the pineapple juice. and blend until smooth.

2. Finely grate the rind from half of the lemon and squeeze the juice. Mix the juice into the yogurt in a large jug, along with the fruit purée and liquid sweetener.

3. Put the ice cubes into the food processor or liquidiser, and pour over the pineapple and yogurt mixture. Blend for 15-30 seconds until it becomes a smooth slush.

4. Divide this mixture between six glasses and top up with lemonade, stirring well with a long handled spoon to blend in the glass.

5. Cut the unpeeled kiwi fruit into thin slices and slit each slice halfway through. Stand each slice of kiwi onto the sides of each glass for decoration.

Step 2 Blend the yogurt, lemon rind and juice, liquid sweetener, and the pineapple and kiwi fruit mixture together in a large jug.

Step 3 Blend together the ice and the pineapple yogurt mixture until it becomes a smooth slush.

Cook's Notes

Time
Preparation takes 5-10 minutes.

Cook's Tip
Do not use set yogurt in this drink as it will not blend smoothly.

Variation
Use orange juice in place of the pineapple juice in this recipe.

SERVES 4

TROPICAL FRUIT HEALTH DRINK

This healthy fruit drink is an ideal breakfast time treat.

3 kiwi fruits
2 ripe nectarines or peaches
2 slices fresh pineapple
1 lime
280ml/½ pint unsweetened pineapple juice
1 kiwi fruit or lime, for decoration

Step 5 Blend the fruit and the juices in a liquidiser or food processor, until smooth.

Step 2 Carefully peel away the skin from the blanched nectarines or peaches, using a sharp knife.

Step 3 Cut the peaches in half and twist them carefully apart to remove the stones.

1. Carefully remove the peel from the kiwi fruit and roughly chop the flesh.

2. Plunge the nectarines or peaches into boiling water for 30 seconds and carefully peel off the blanched skins.

3. Halve the peaches or nectarines, and remove the stones. Chop the flesh and put this into a liquidiser or food processor, along with the kiwi fruit.

4. Remove the peel from the pineapple slices and cut into quarters. Cut away the tough core from the pineapple and add the remaining flesh to the kiwi and peaches in the liquidiser or food processor.

5. Squeeze the juice from the lime and add this, with the pineapple juice, to the fruit in the food processor. Blend until smooth, and pour into individual serving glasses.

6. Decorate the edge of the glasses with thin slices of un-peeled kiwi fruit or lime.

Cook's Notes

Time
Preparation takes approximately 10 minutes.

Variation
Add 280ml/½ pint sugar-free lemonade to this recipe for a lighter more refreshing fruit drink.

Serving Idea
Serve spooned over muesli for a refreshing breakfast.

SERVES 4-6
SPICED MANGO JUICE

Fresh mango juice is not easily available in shops, but is so easy to make that it is well worth producing your own.

3 large ripe mangoes
1.25ml/½ tsp ground ginger
1.25ml/½ tsp ground cinnamon
280ml/½ pint unsweetened orange juice
1 lemon
1 orange for decoration

1. Peel the mangoes and cut the flesh away from the stone.

2. Put the mango flesh into a liquidiser or food processor along with the spices and orange juice. Blend until smooth.

3. Cut the lemon in half and squeeze the juice.

4. Add enough lemon juice to the mango purée to suit your own preference.

5. Pour the mango juice into individual serving glasses.

6. Slice the orange thinly and use these to decorate the sides of the glass.

Step 1 Carefully cut away the mango flesh from the long inside stone using a sharp knife.

Step 2 Blend the fruit, spices and orange juice together in a liquidiser or food processor, until they are smooth.

Cook's Notes

Time
Preparation takes about 15 minutes.

Cook's Tip
Use this drink, mixed with 140ml/¼ pint dark rum for an unusual cocktail.

Variation
Add 1 large peeled banana to the mango mixture before puréeing for a thicker, and more filling breakfast drink.

INDEX